ENDLESS ————————————
MAP GALLERY
BOOK OF ASIA

Presented By : ENDLESS

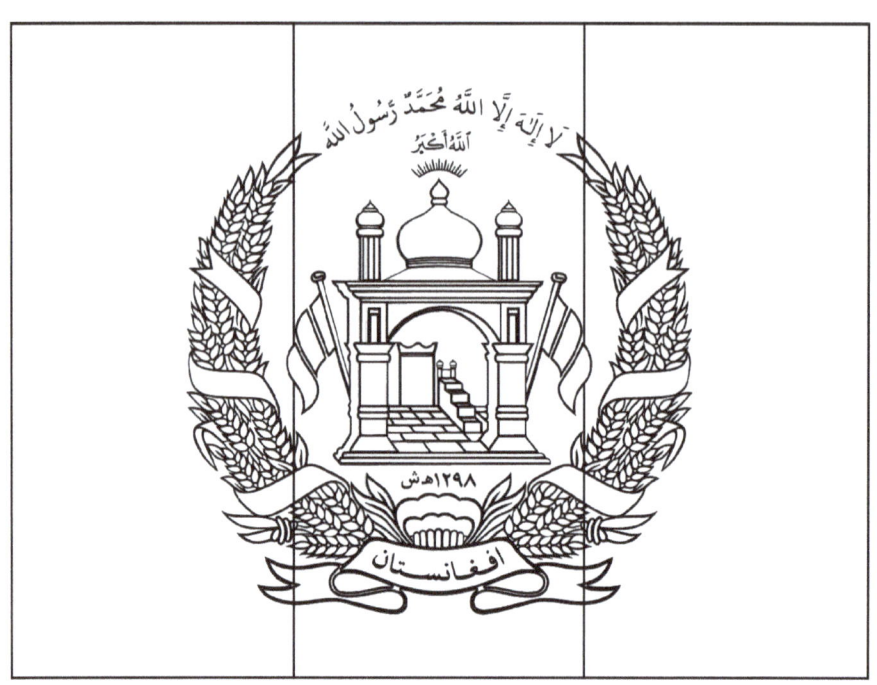

AFGHANISTAN

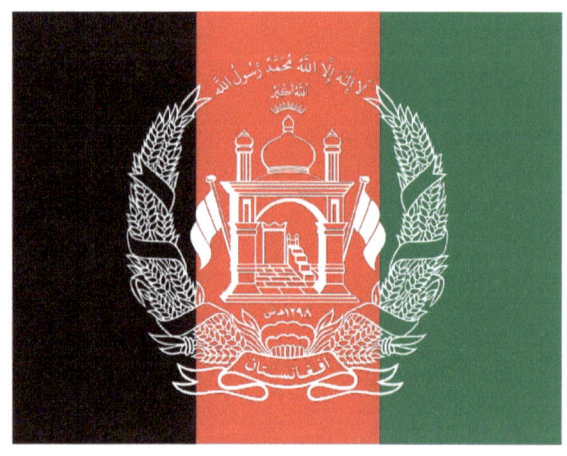

ARMENIA

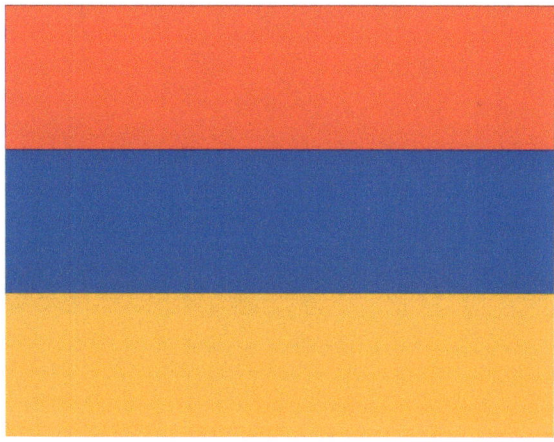

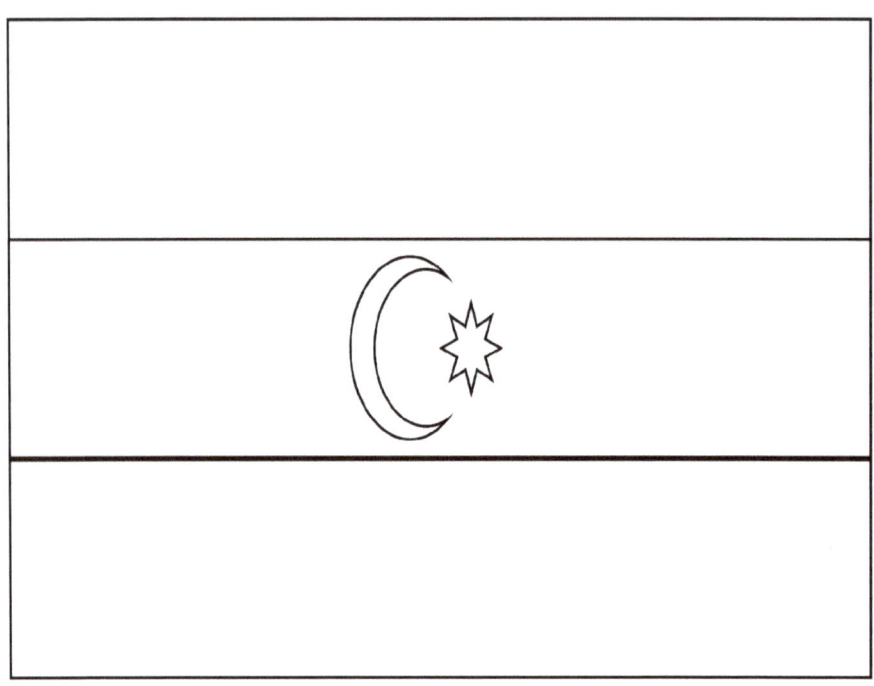

AZERBAIJAN

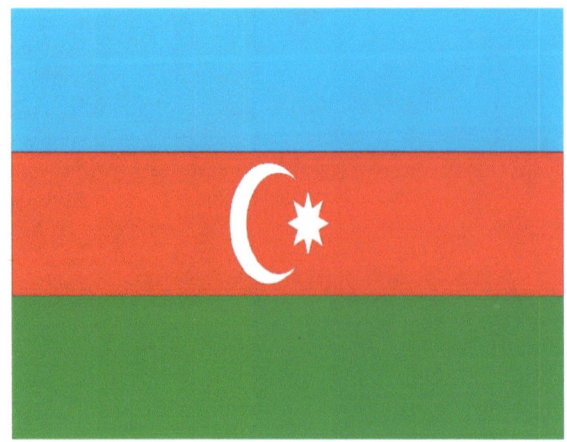

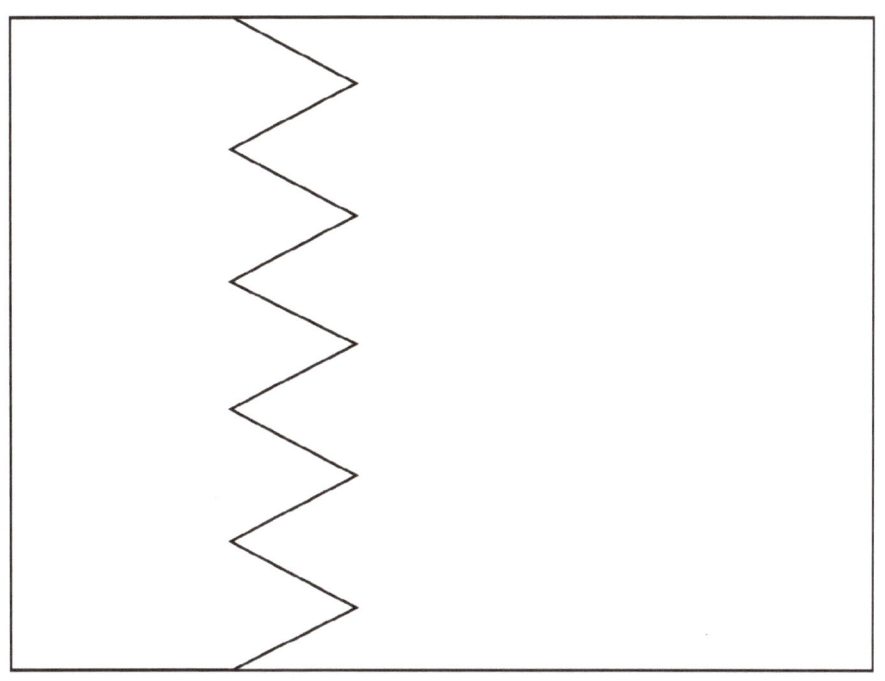

BAHRAIN

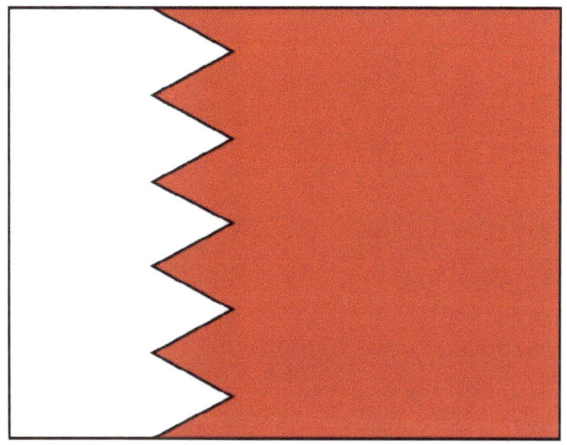

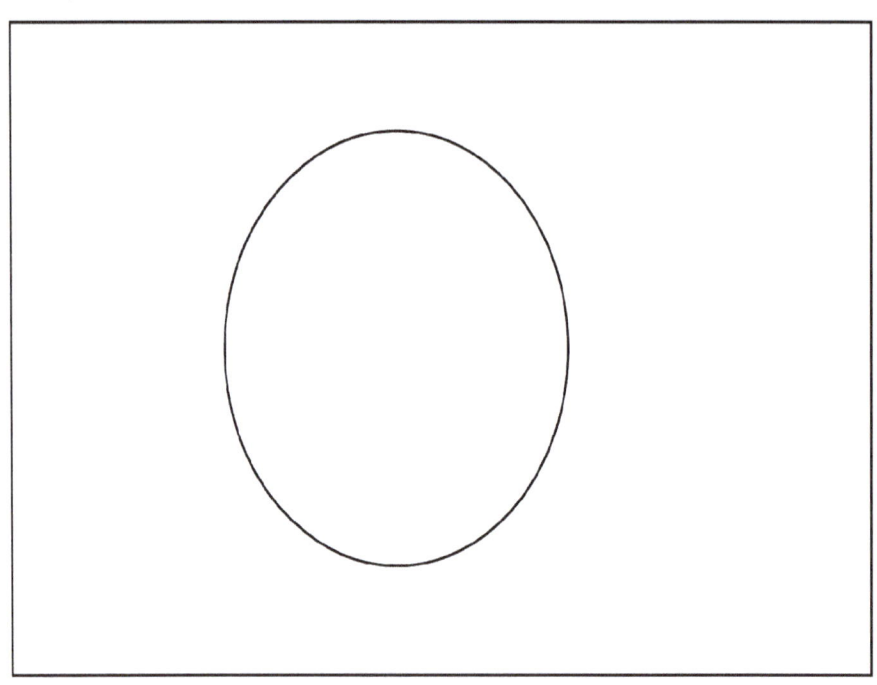

BANGLADESH

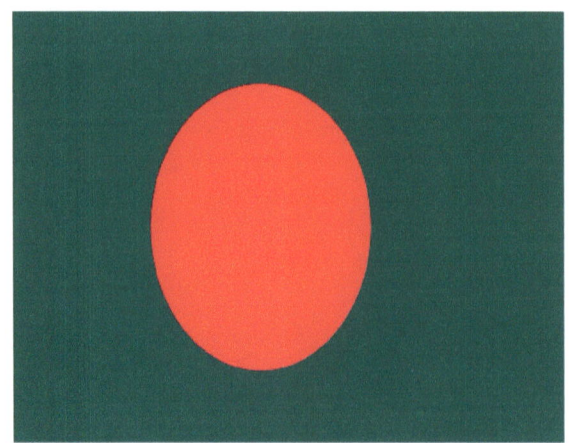

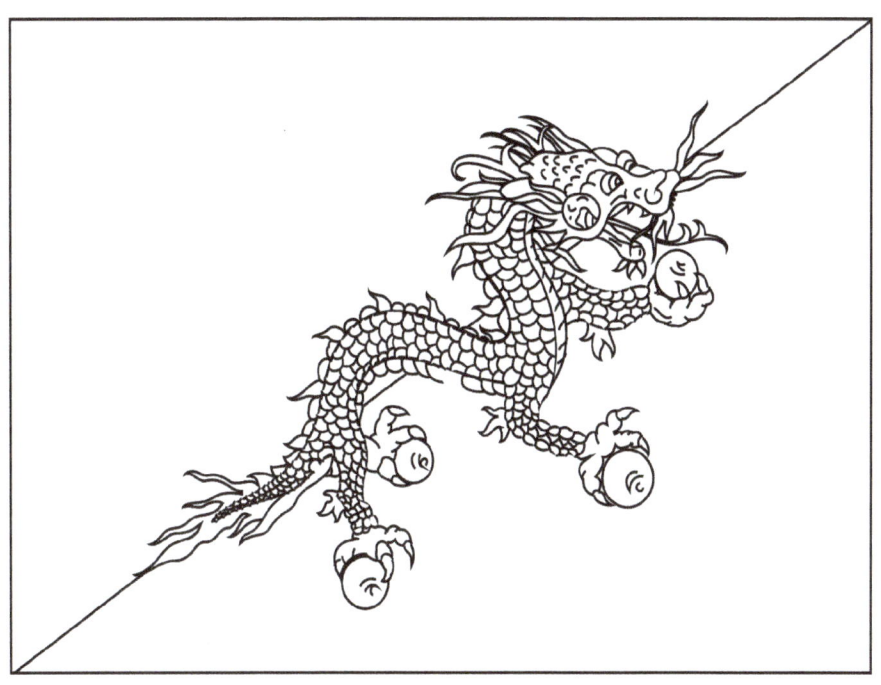

BHUTAN

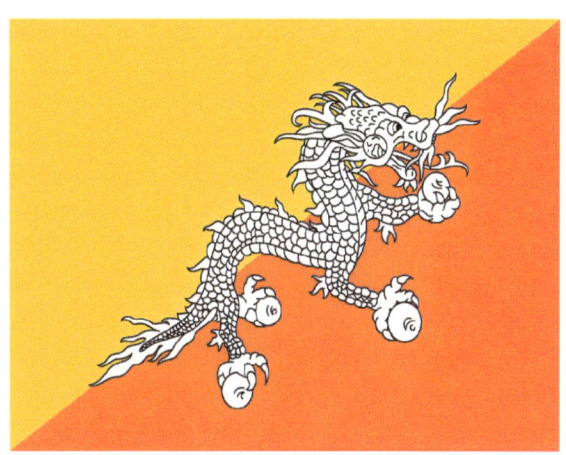

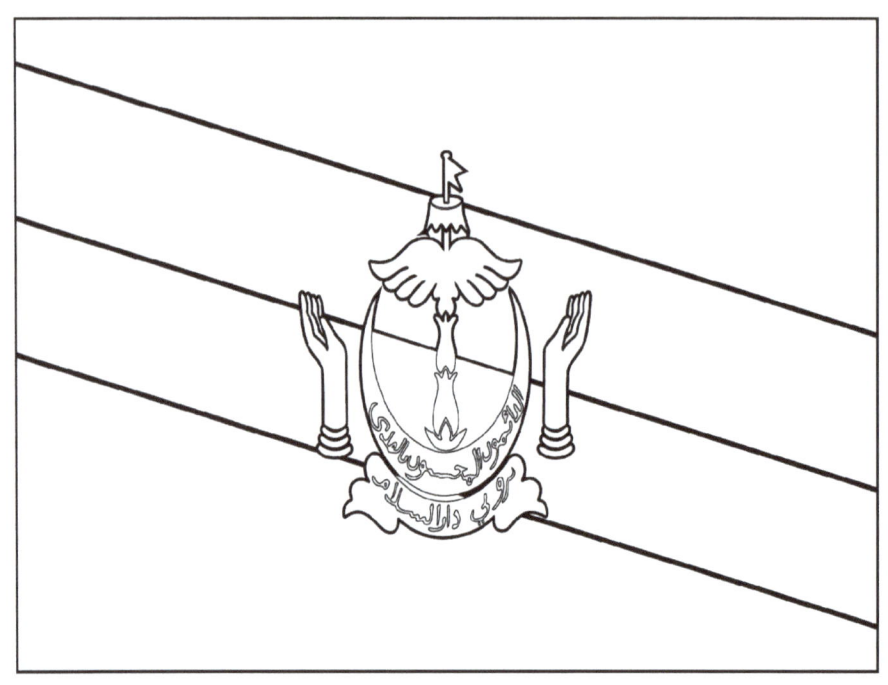

BRUNEI

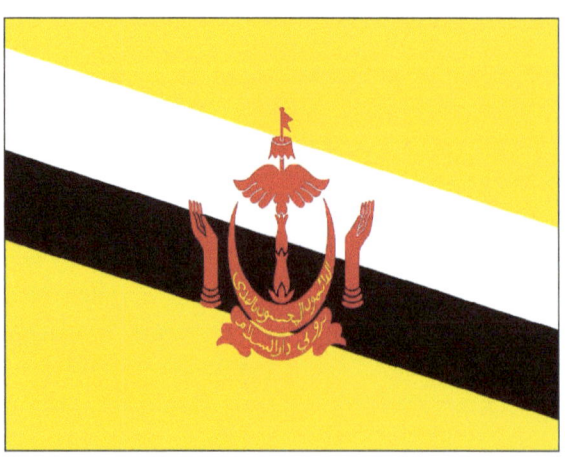

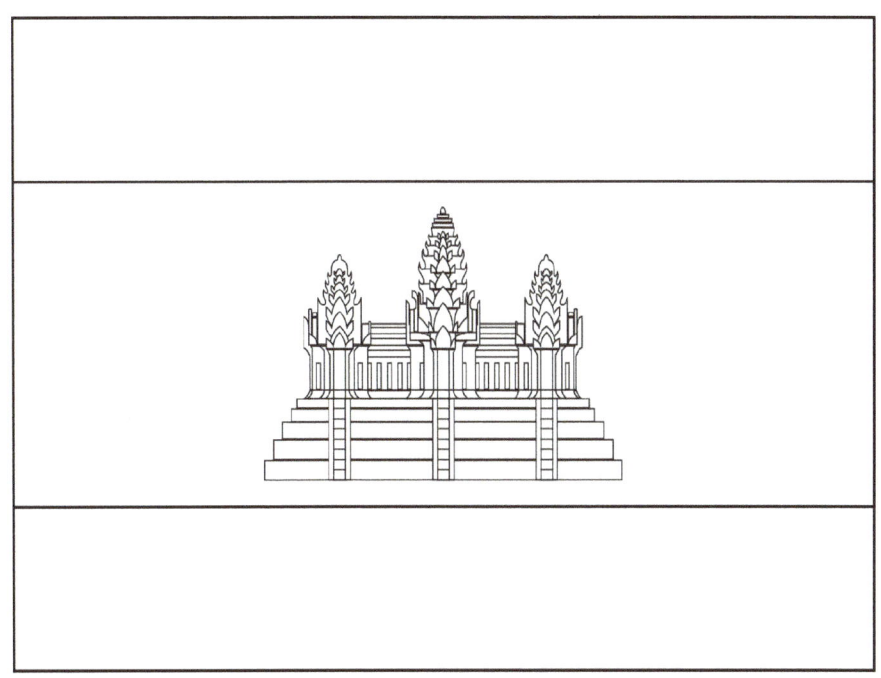

CAMBODIA

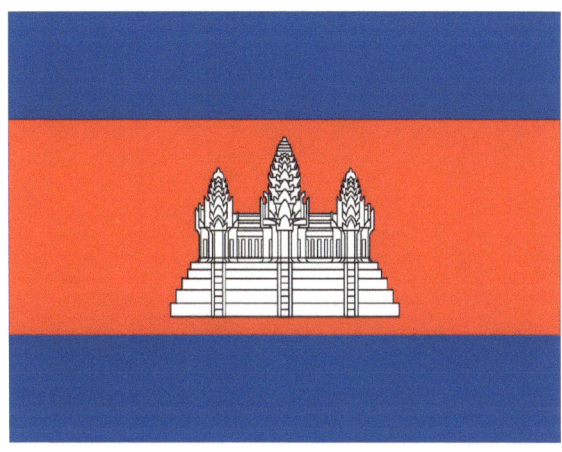

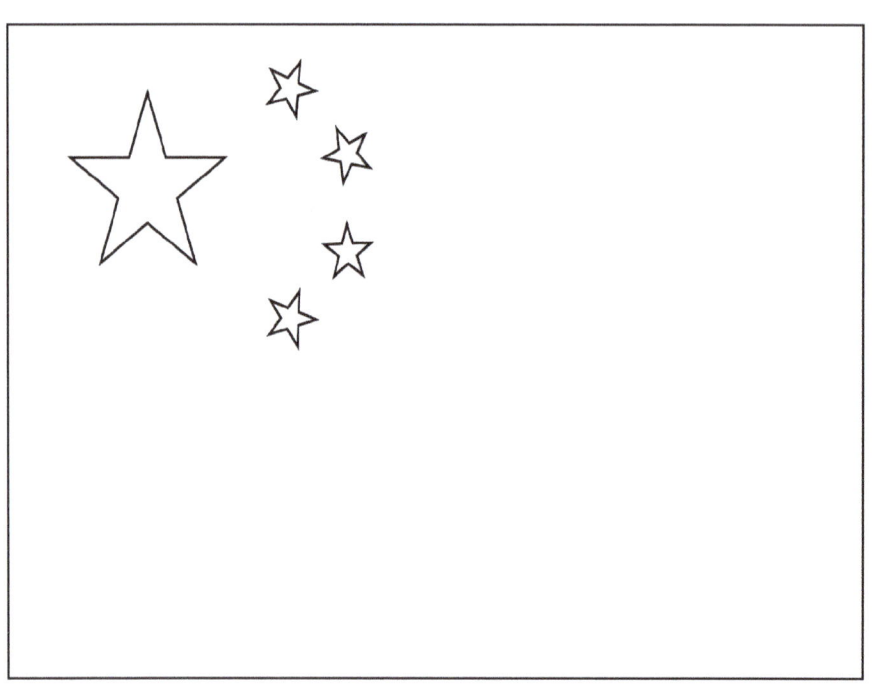

CHINA

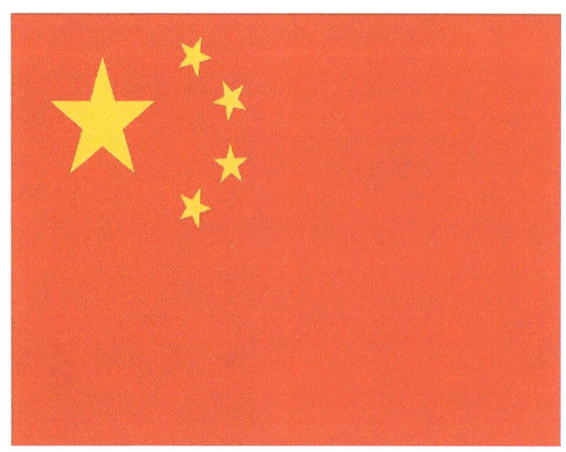

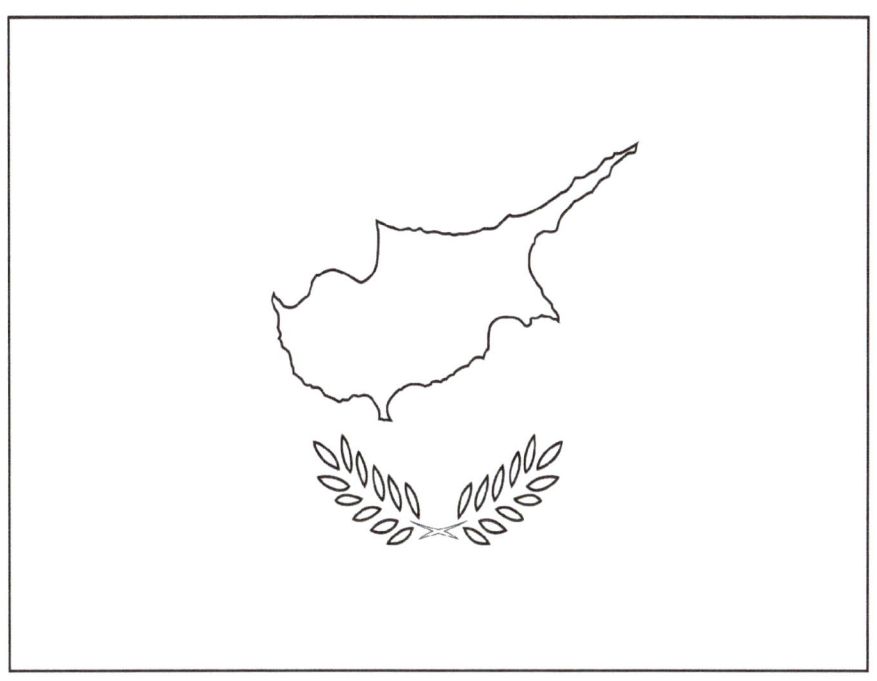

CYPRUS

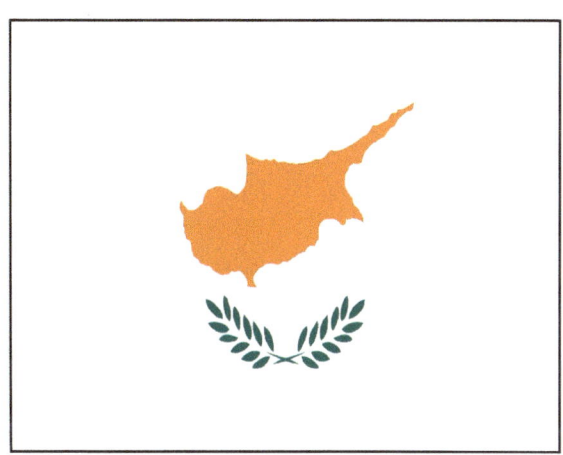

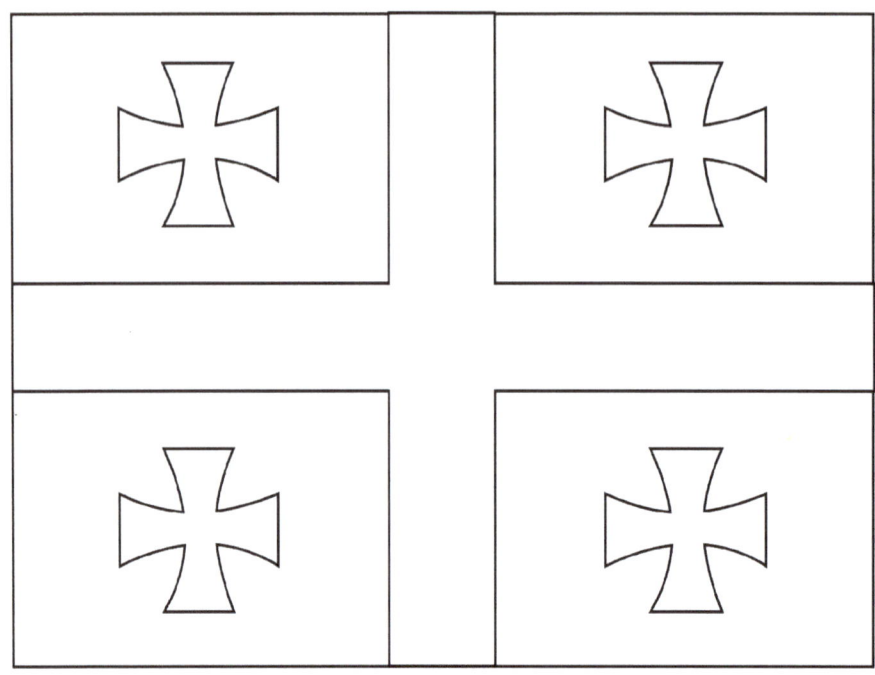

GEORGIA

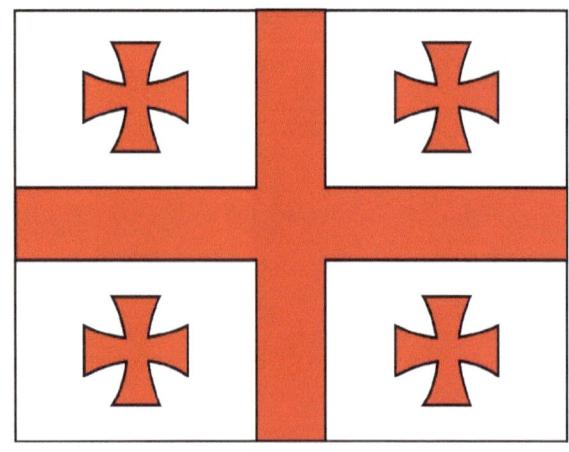

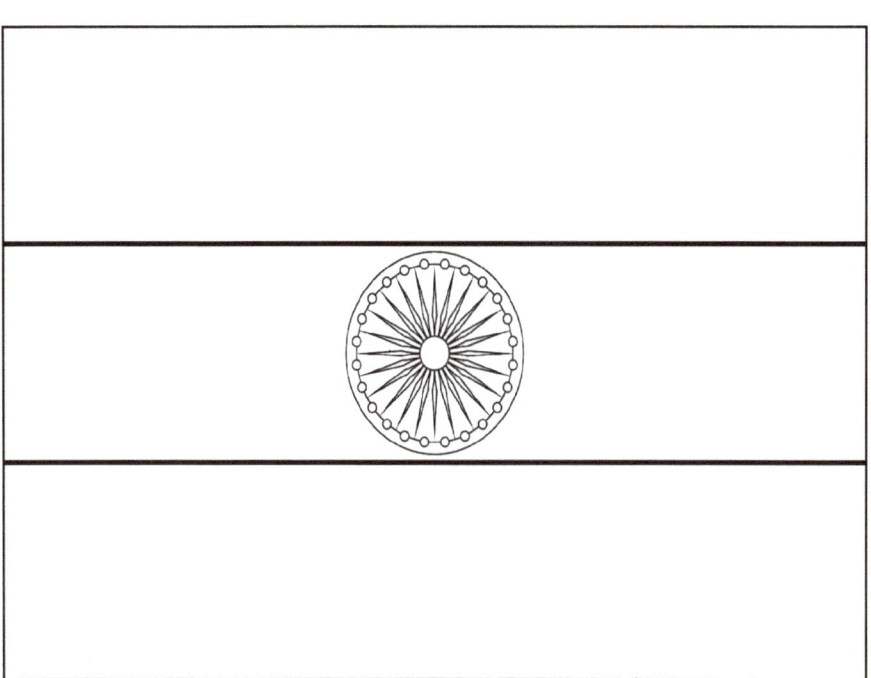

INDIA

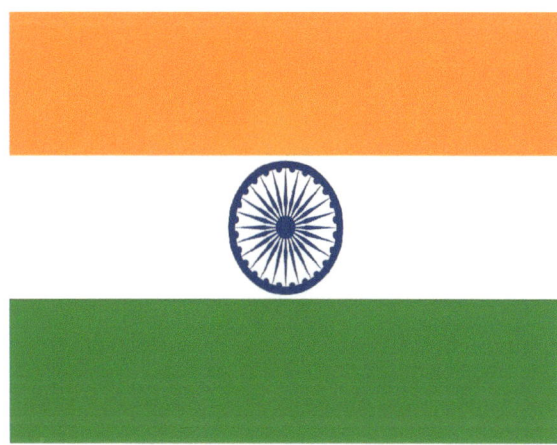

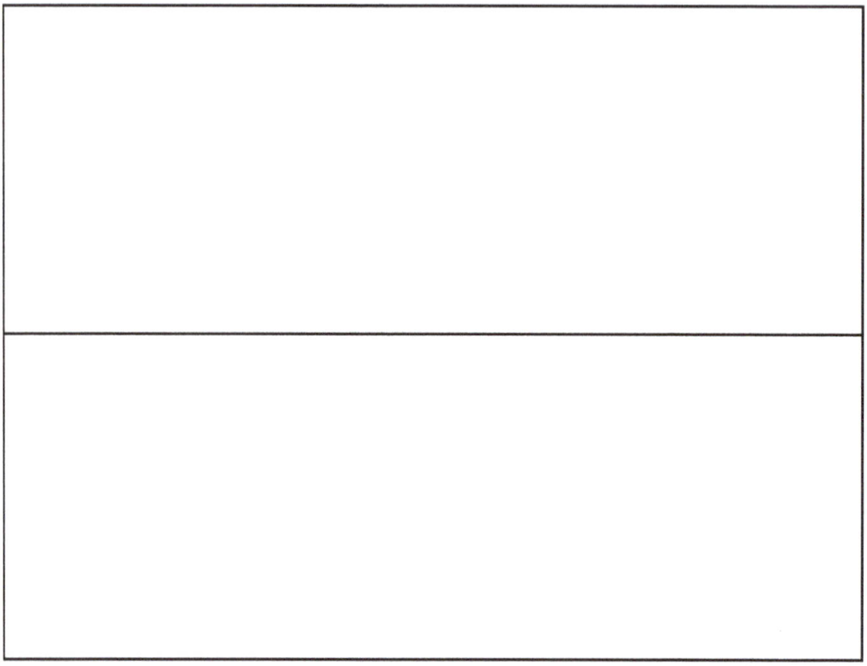

INDONESIA

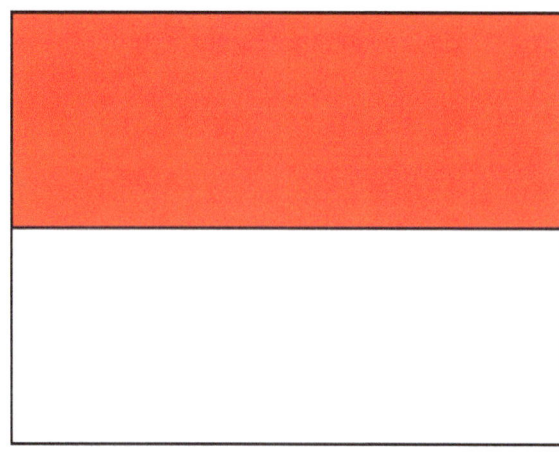

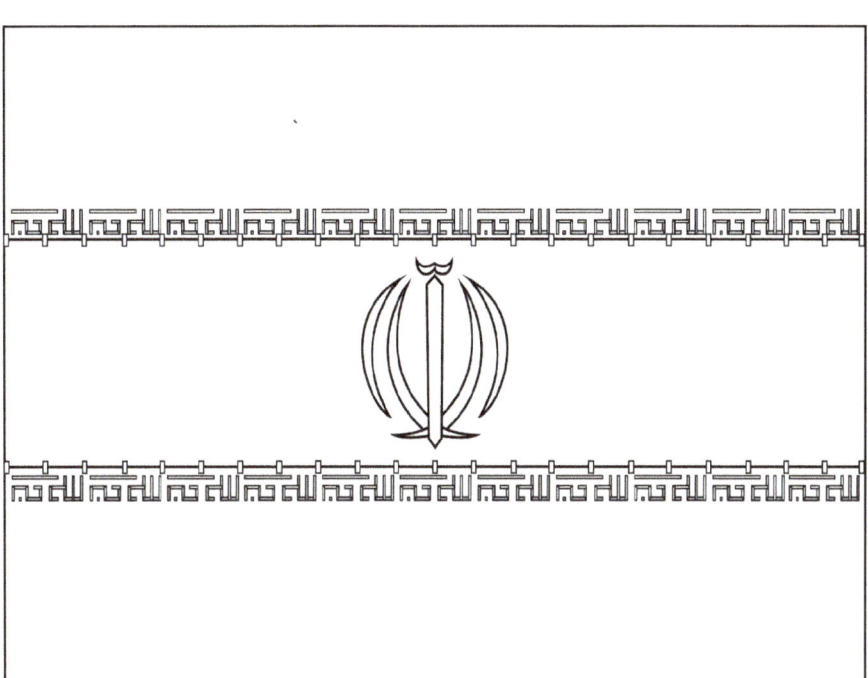

IRAN

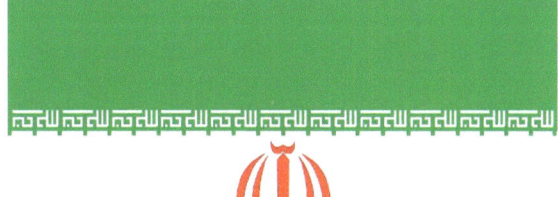

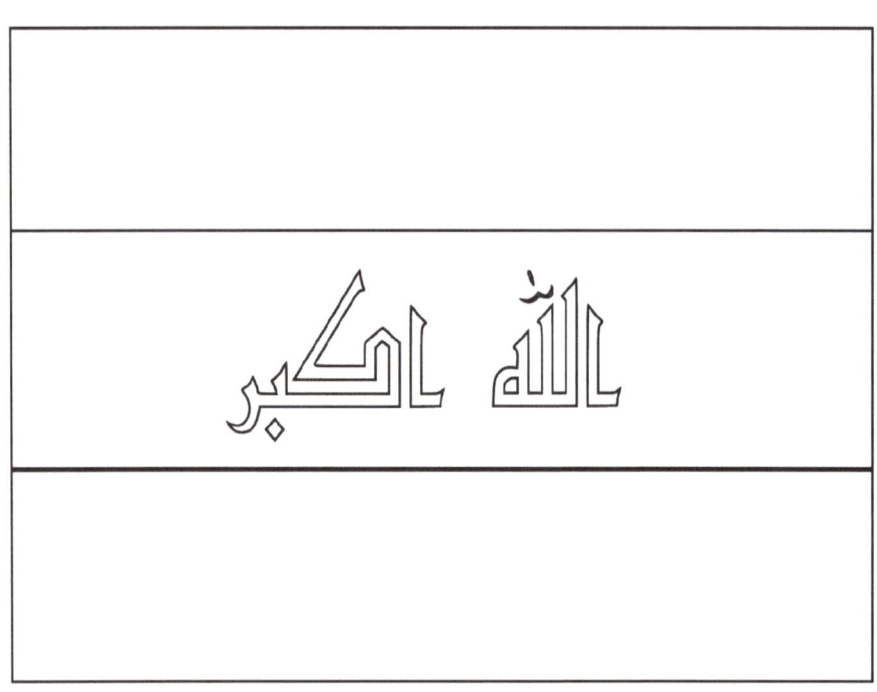

IRAQ

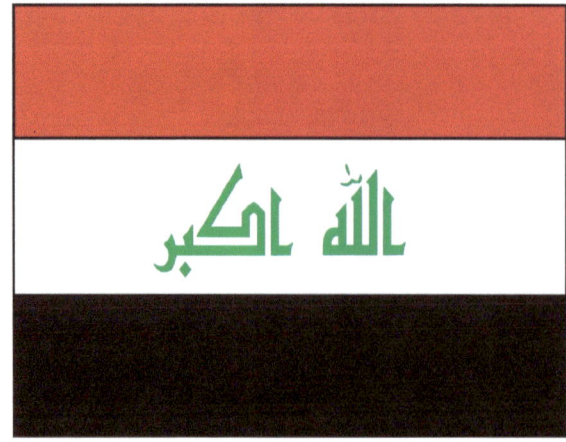

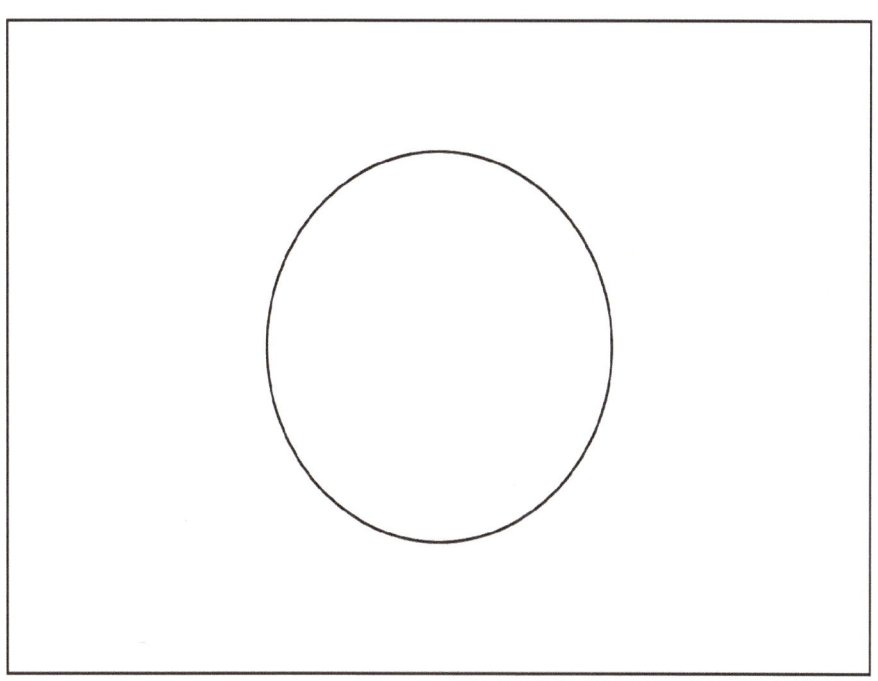

JAPAN

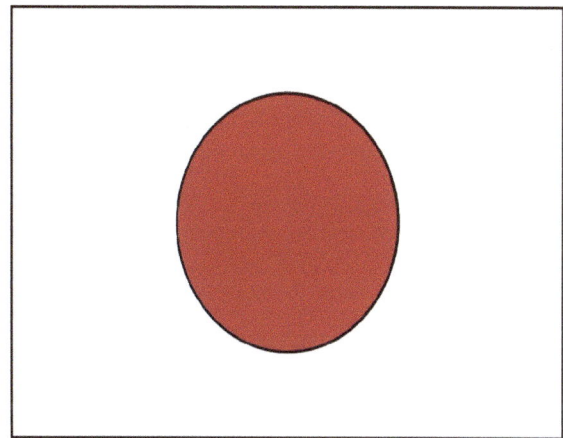

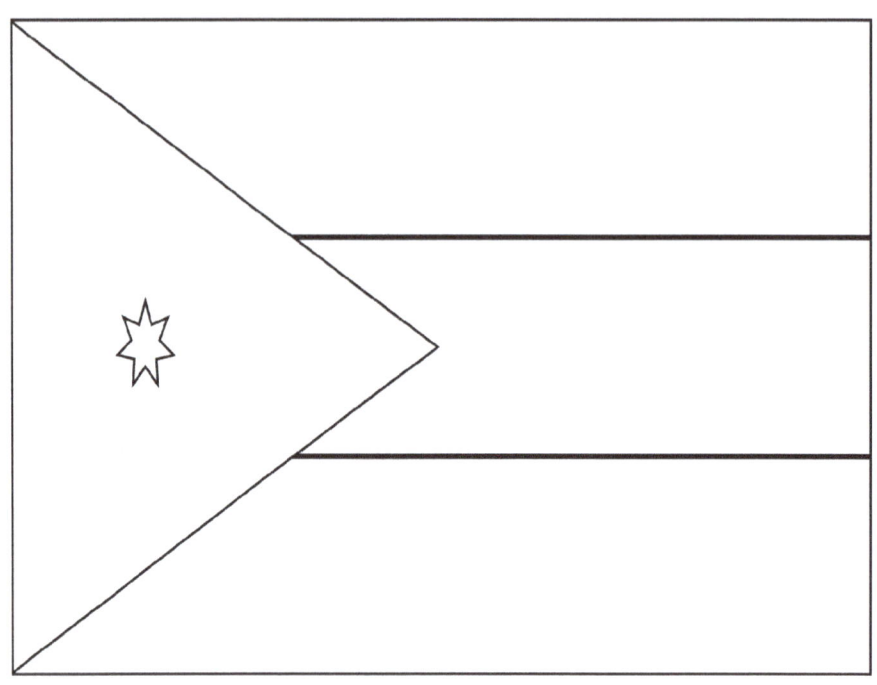

JORDAN

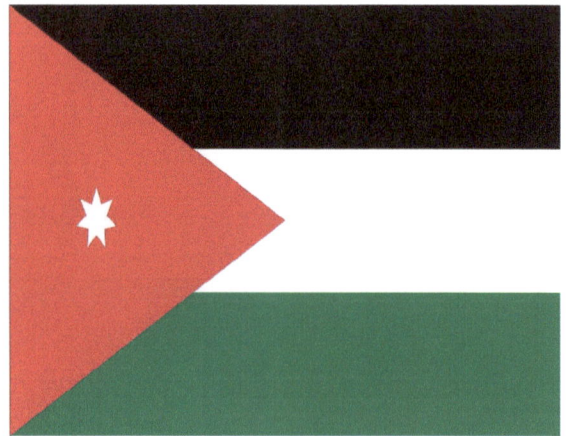

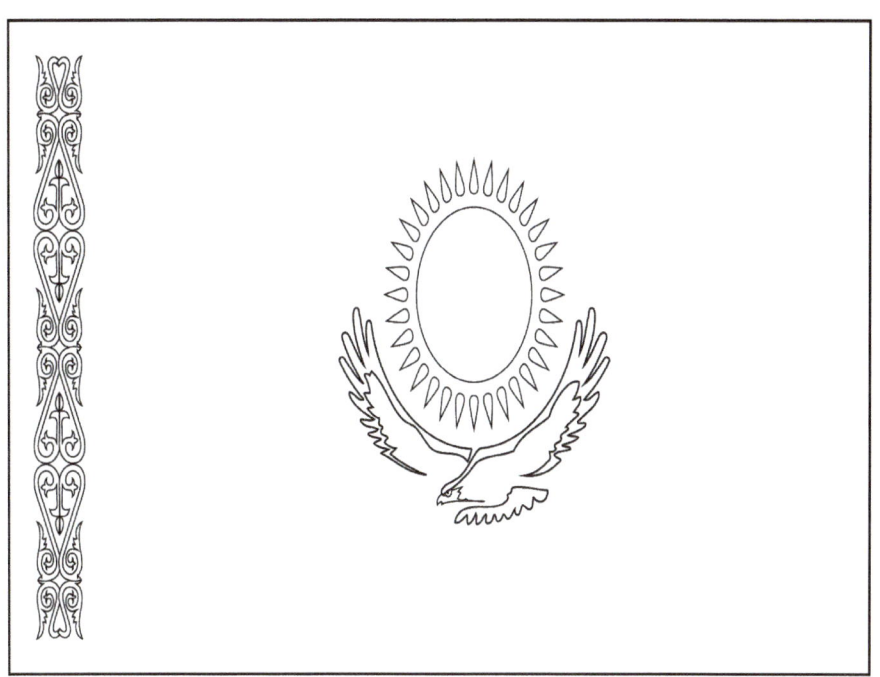

KAZAKHSTAN

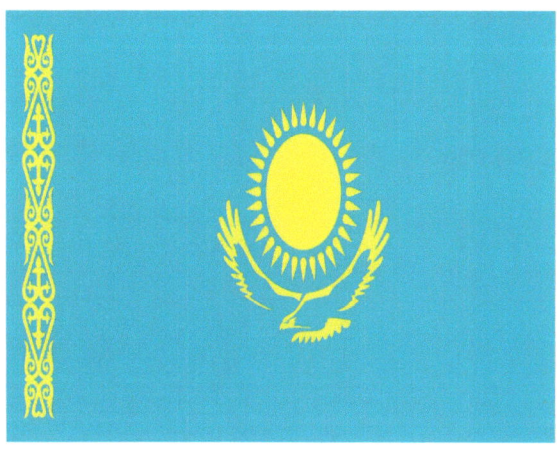

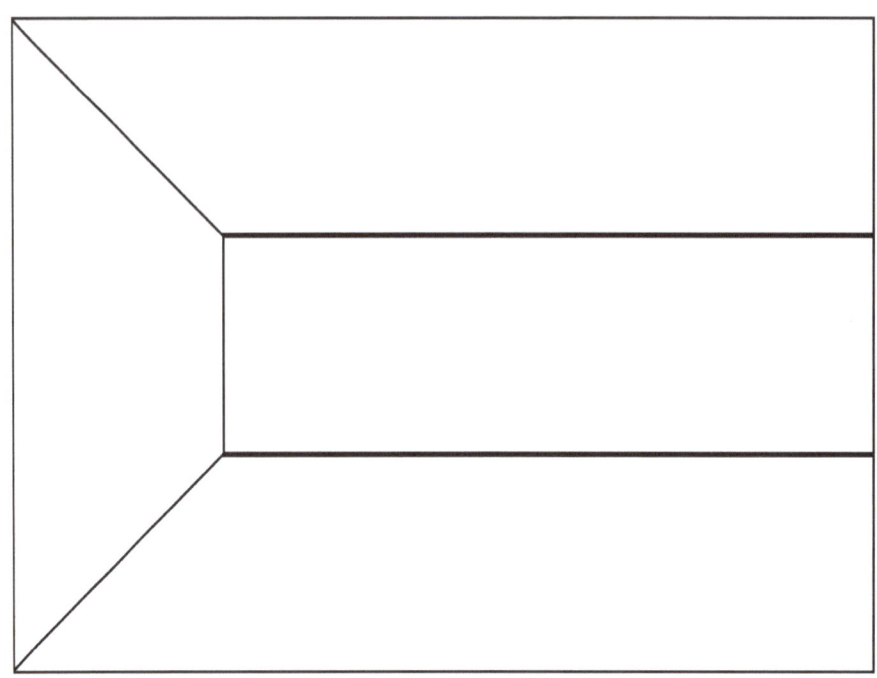

KUWAIT

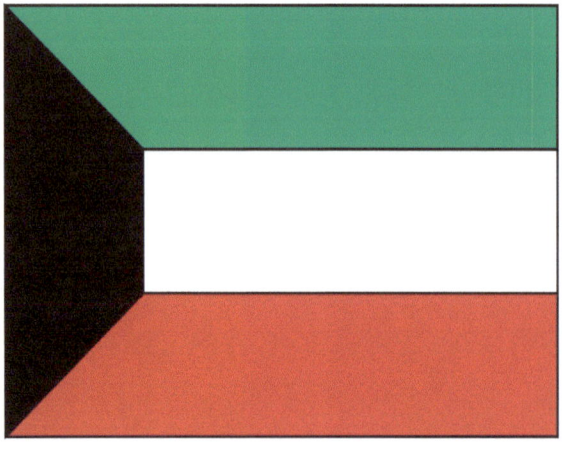

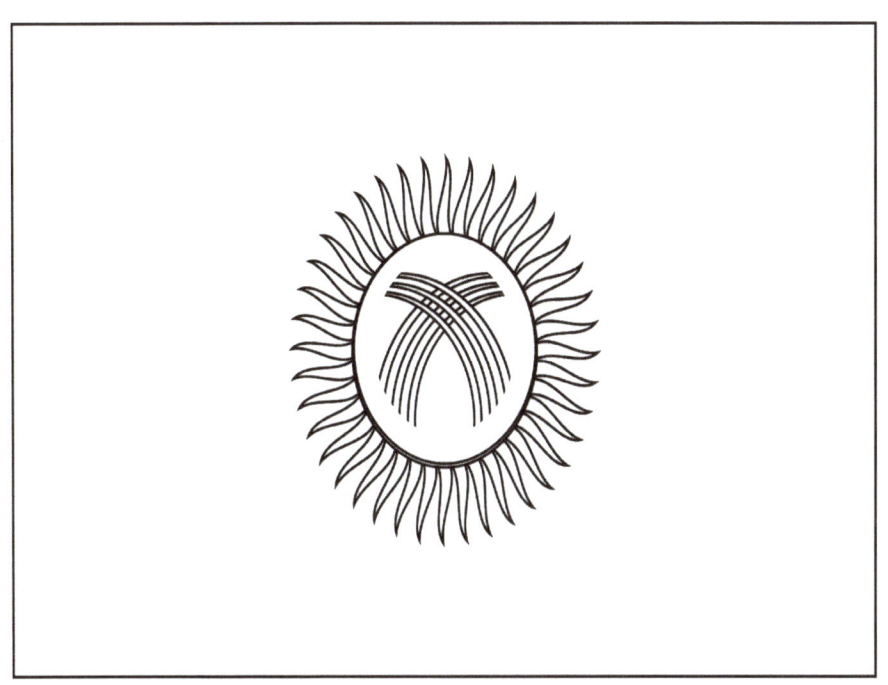

KRYGYZSTAN

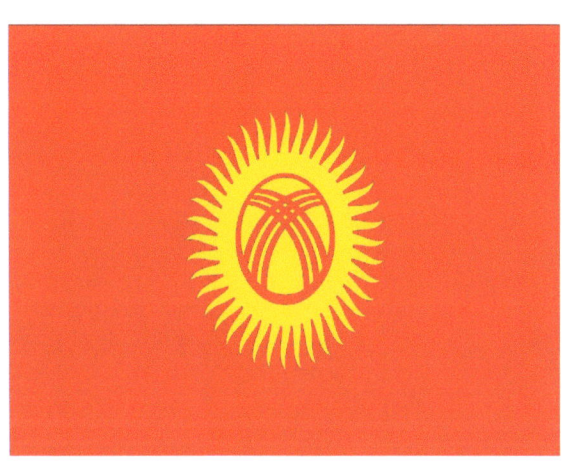

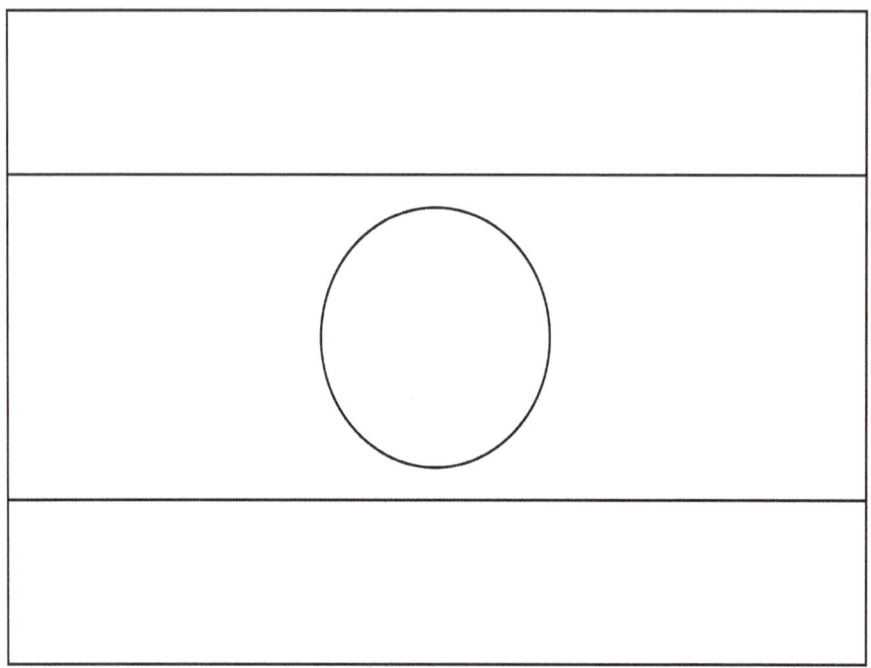

LAOS

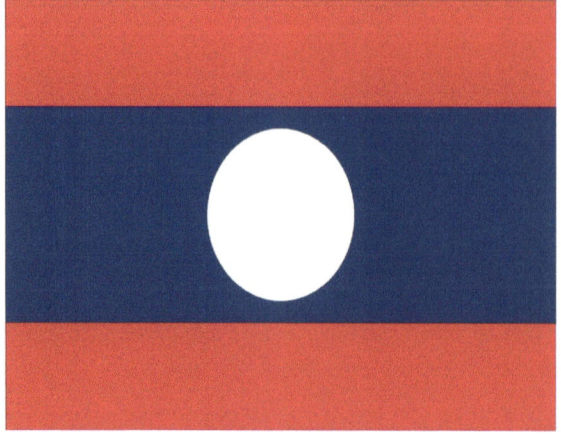

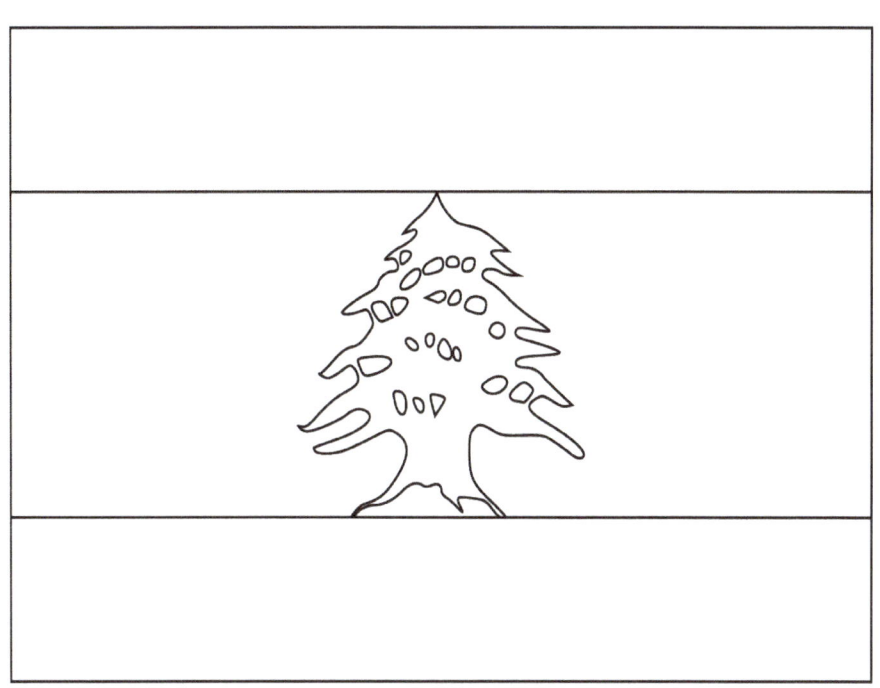

LEBANON

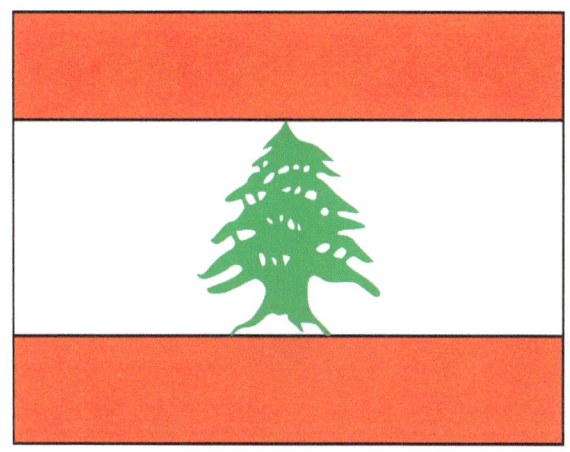

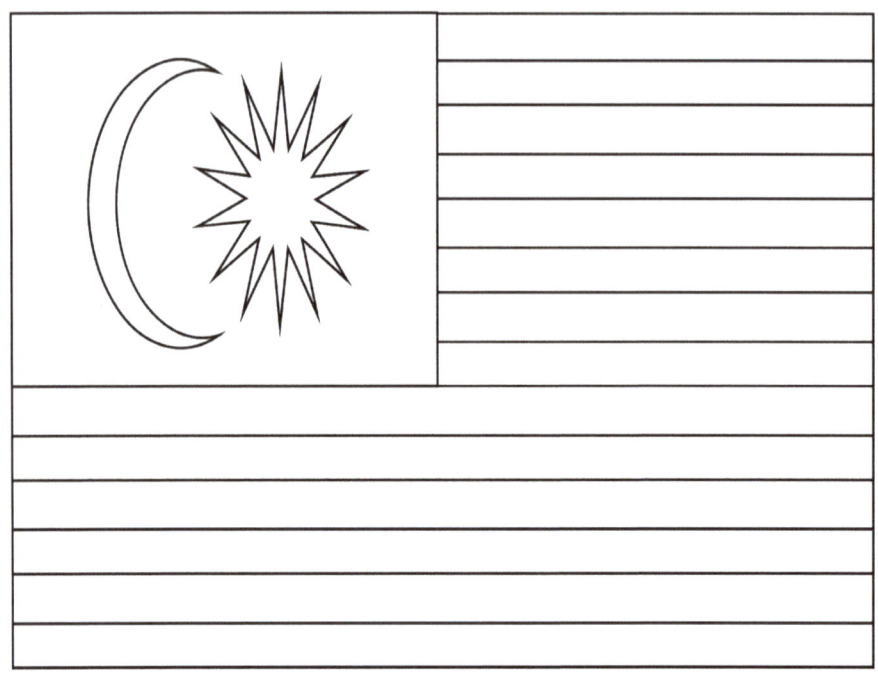

MALAYSIA

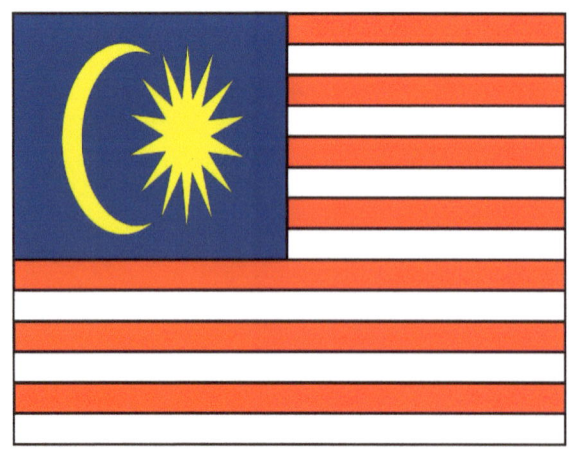

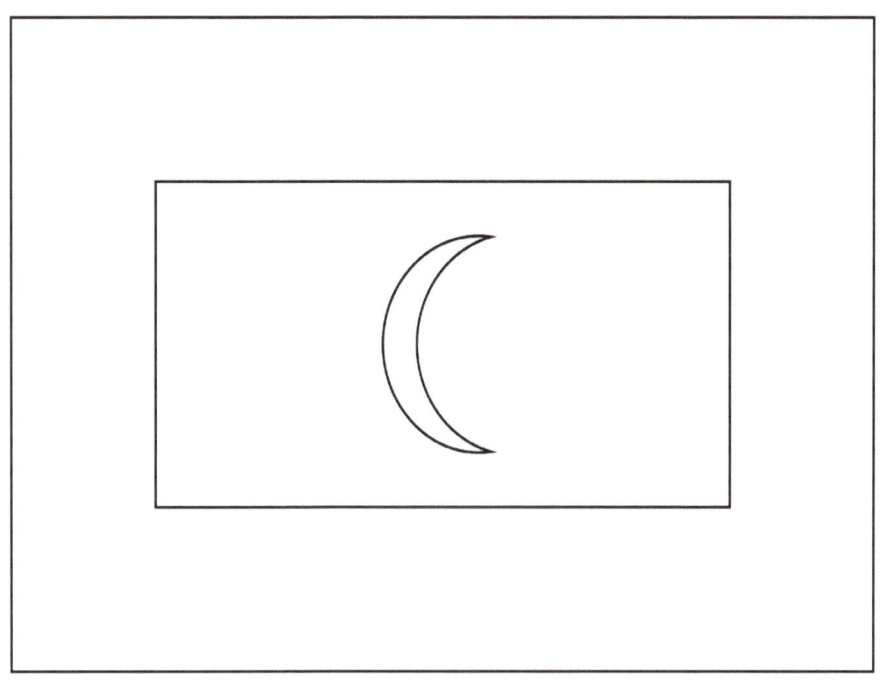

MALDIVES

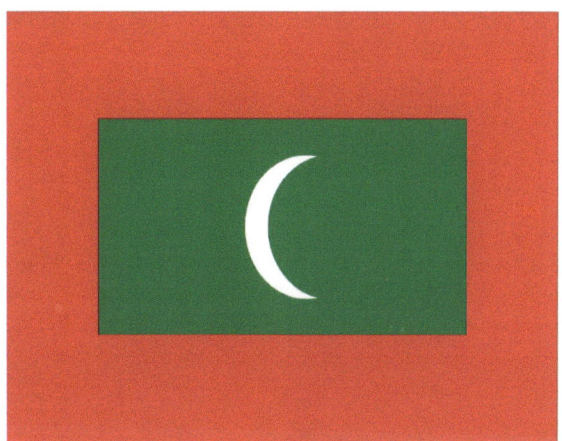

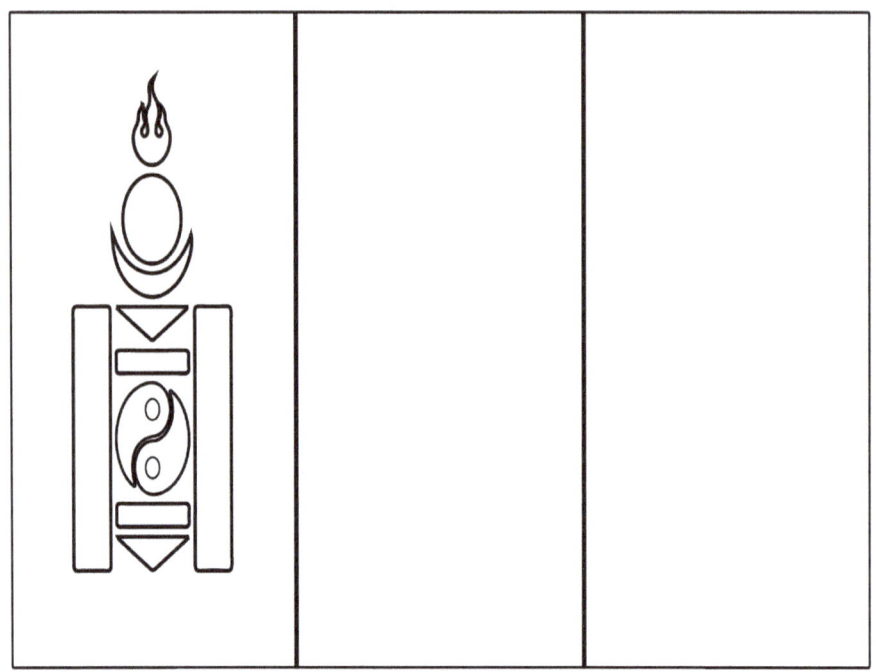

MONGOLIA

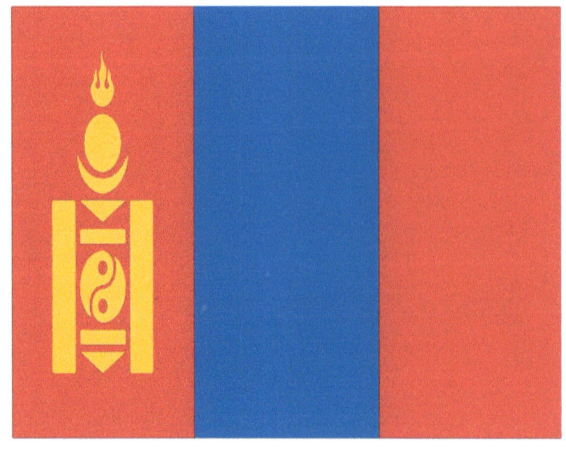

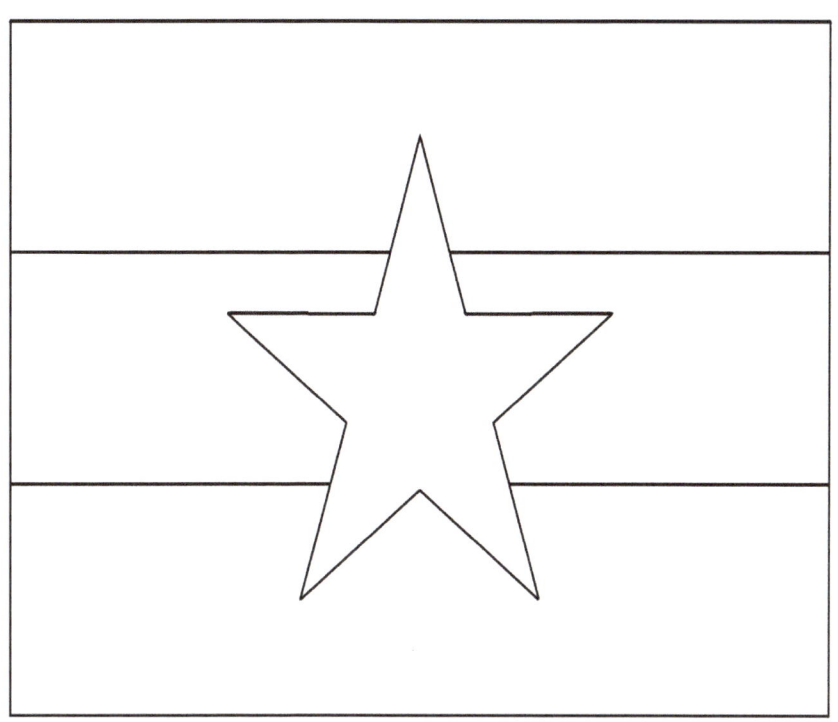

MYANMAR

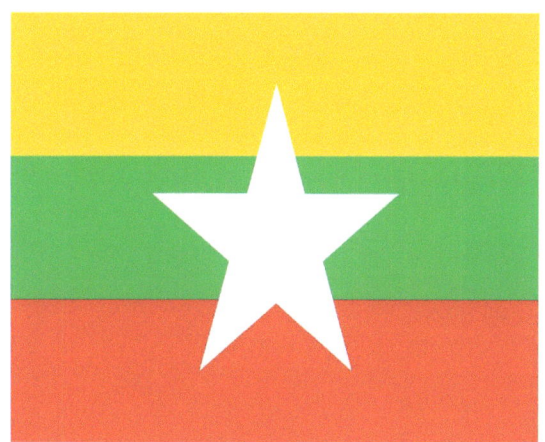

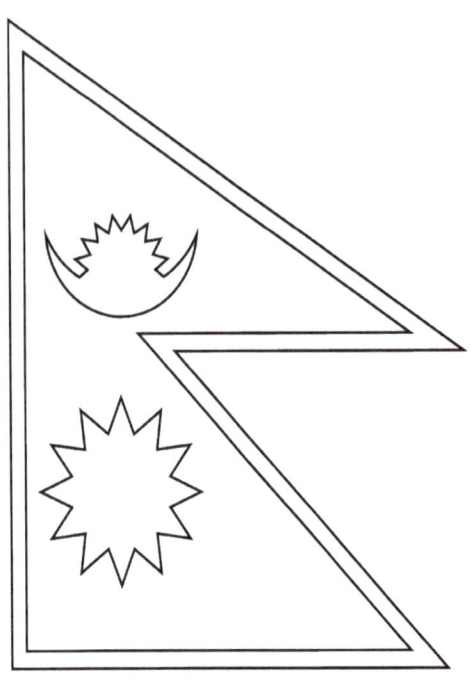

NEPAL

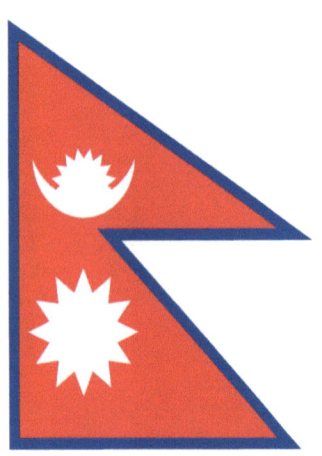

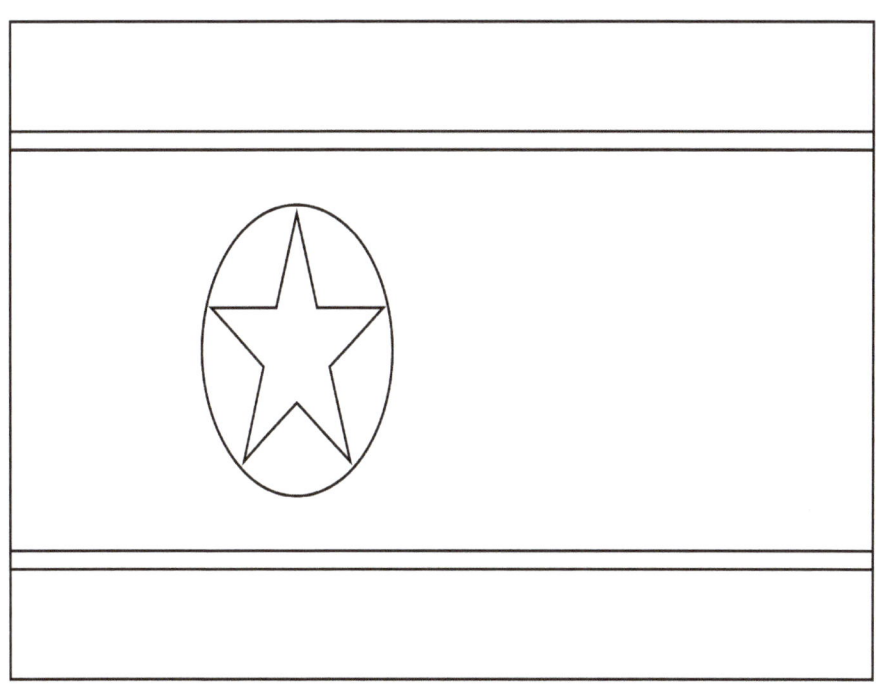

NORTH KOREA

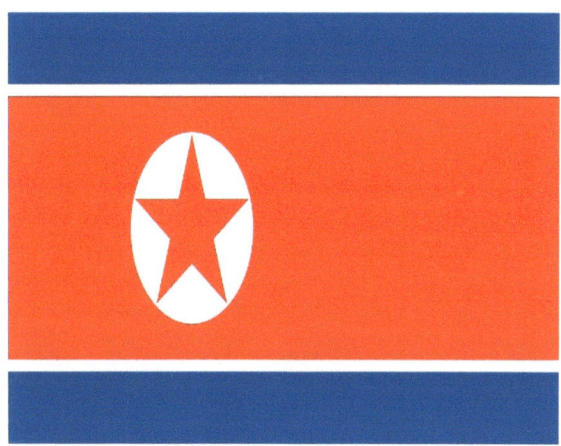

OMAN

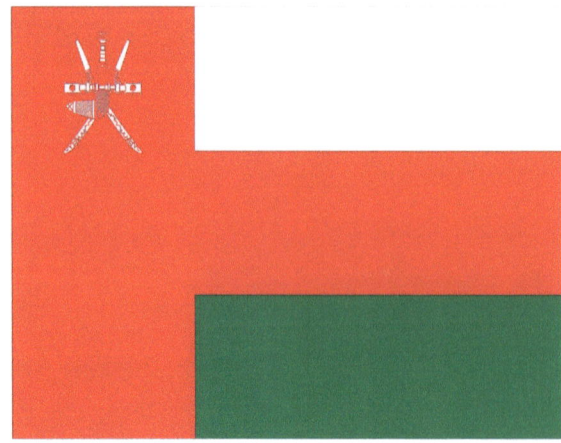

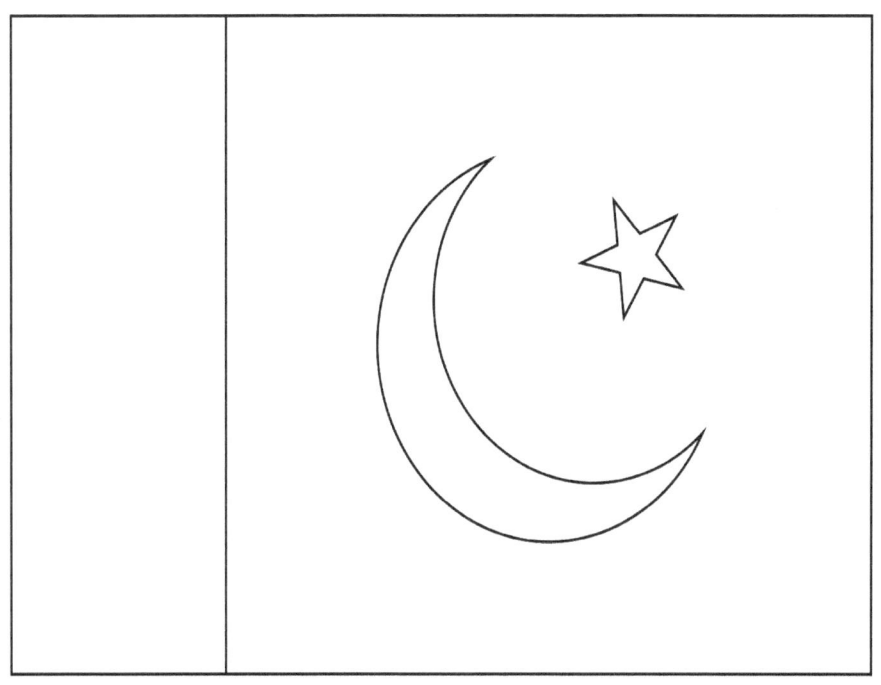

PAKISTAN

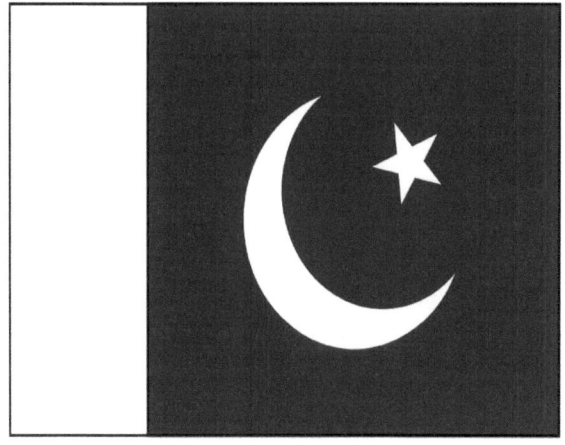

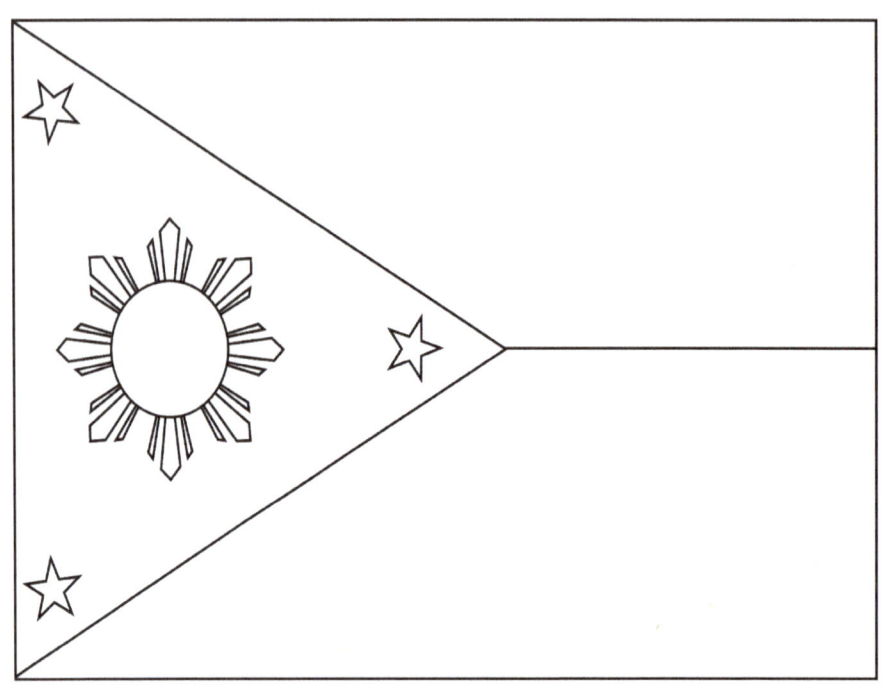

PHILIPPINES

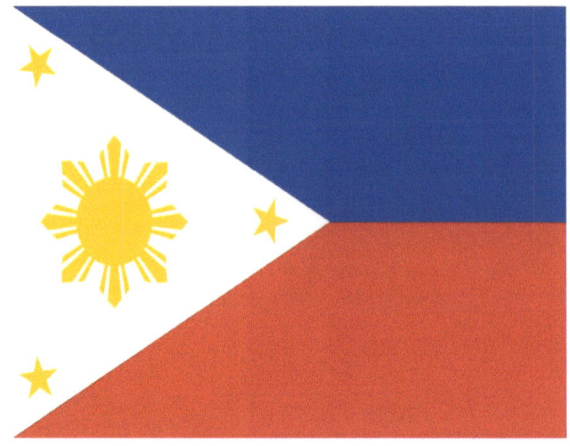

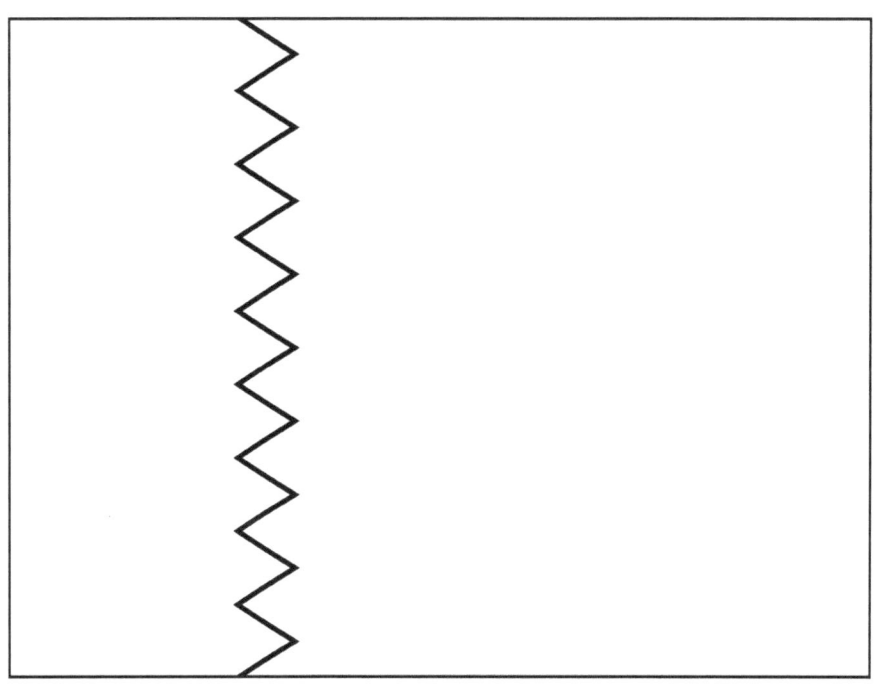

QATAR

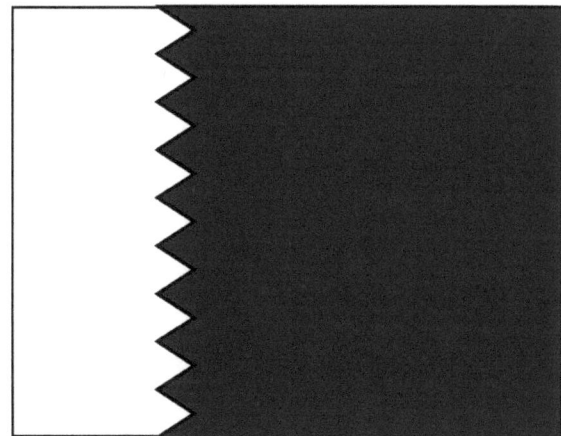

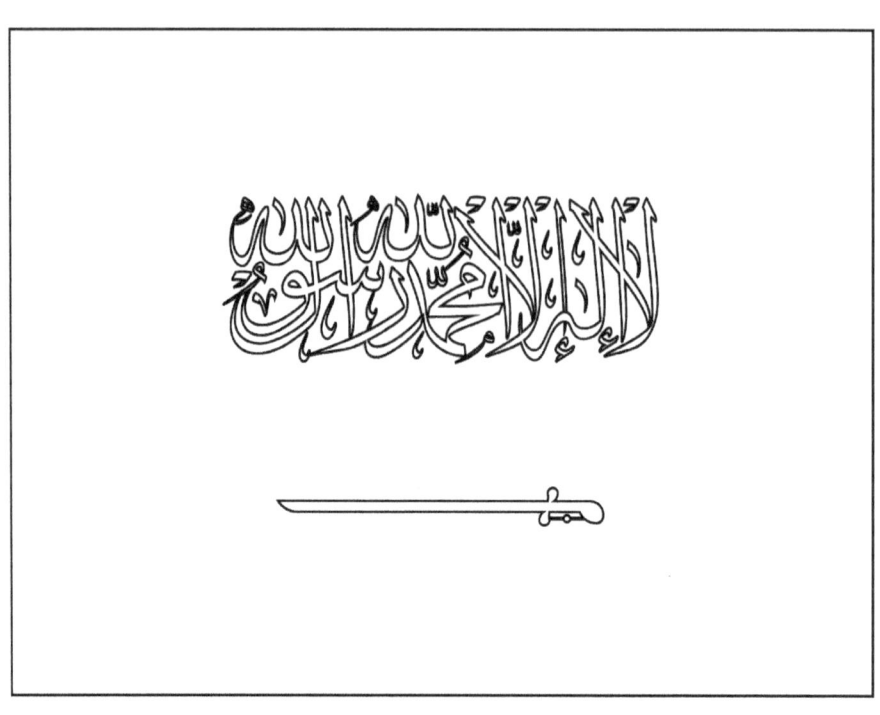

SAUDI ARABIA

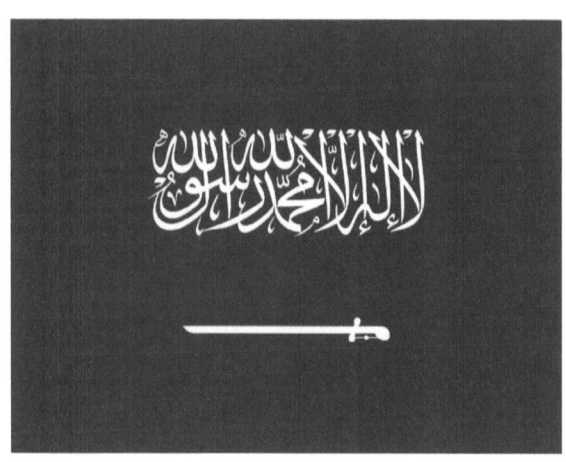

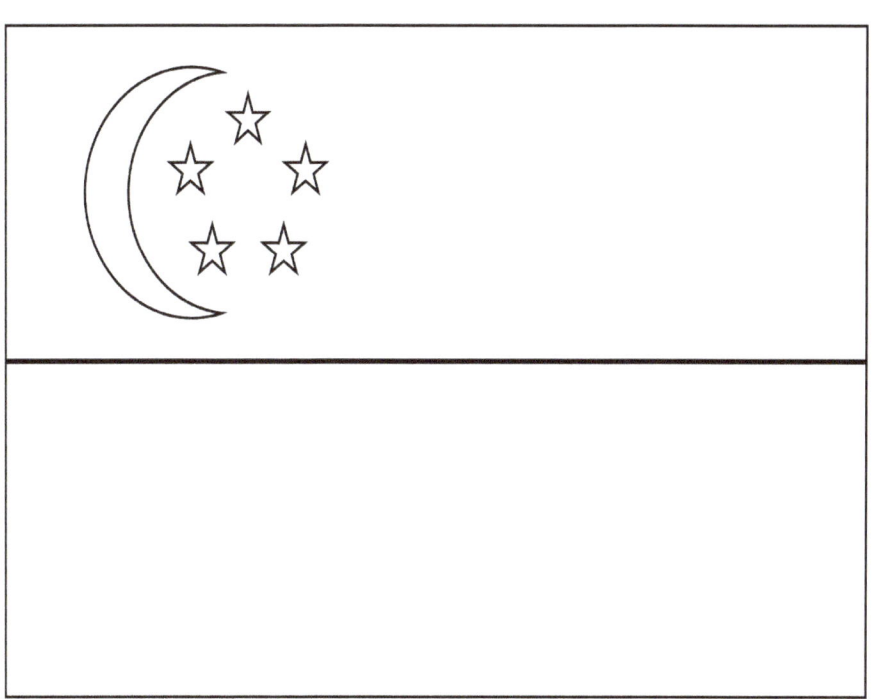

SINGAPORE

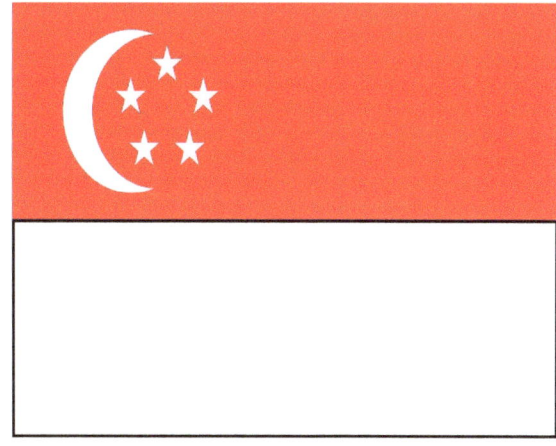

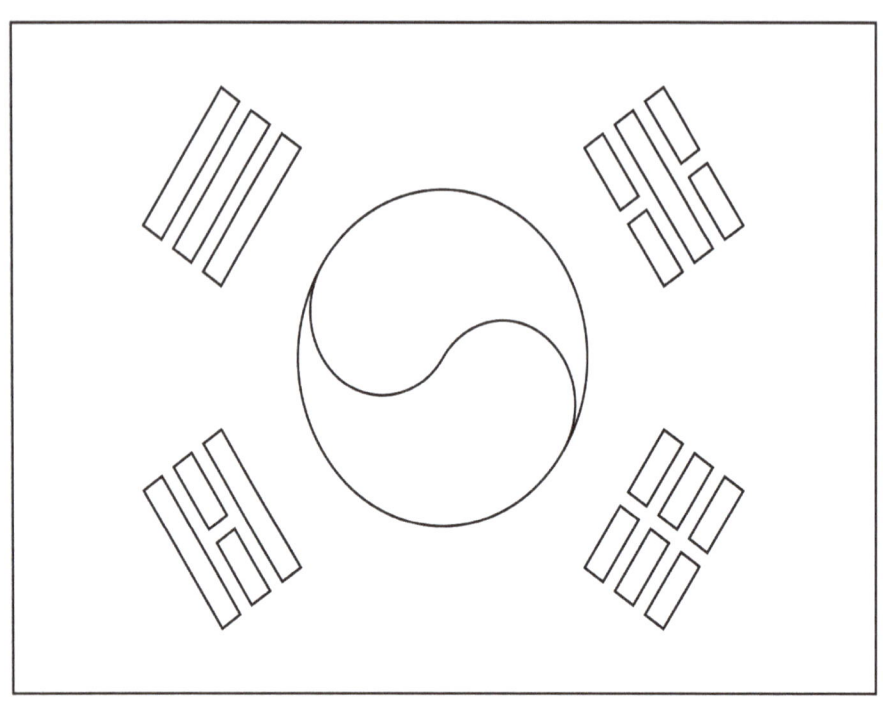

SOUTH KOREA

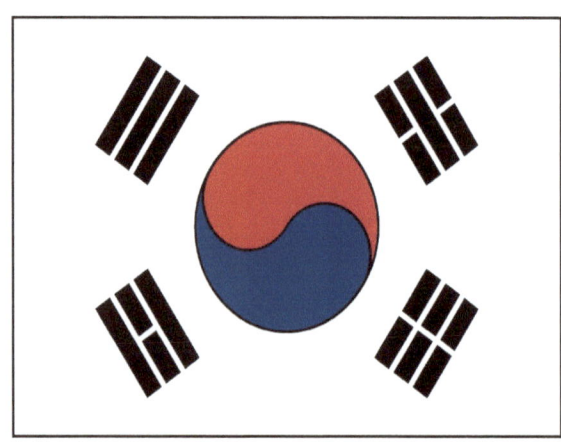

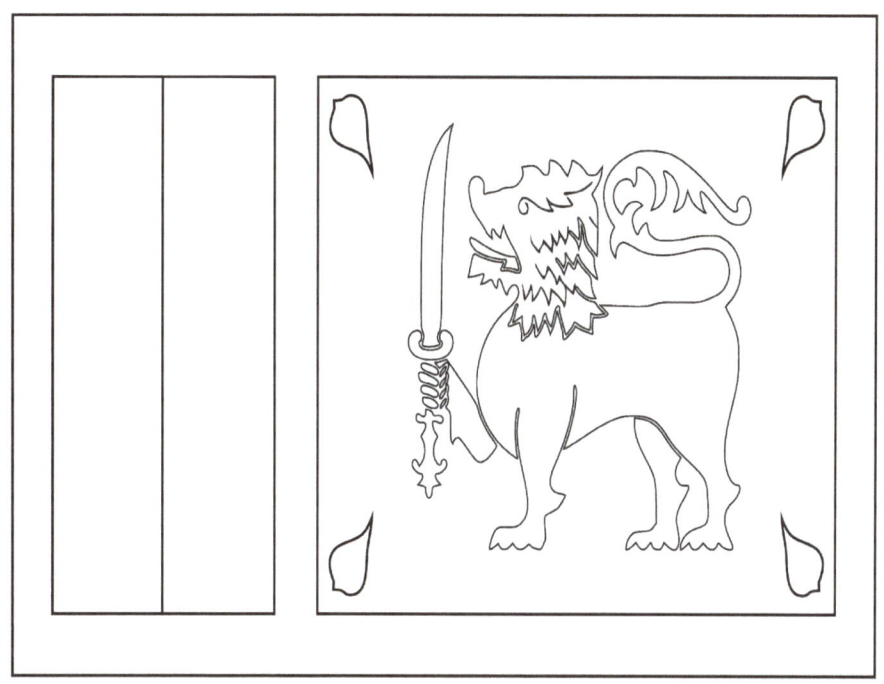

SRI LANKA

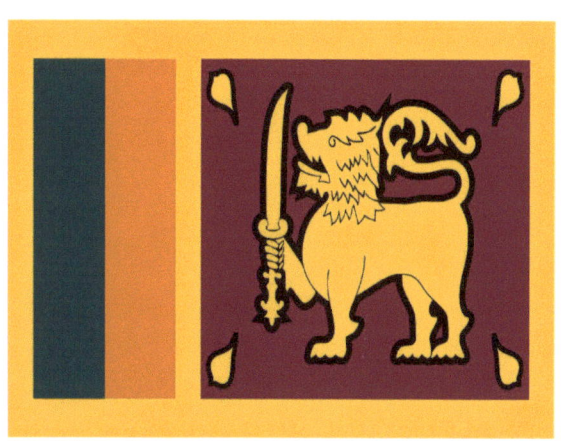

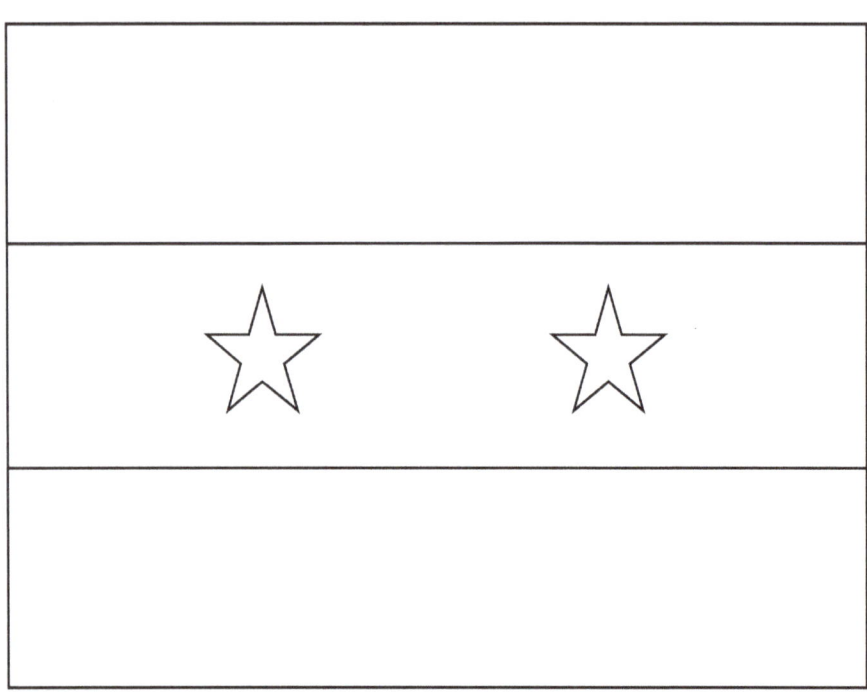

SYRIA

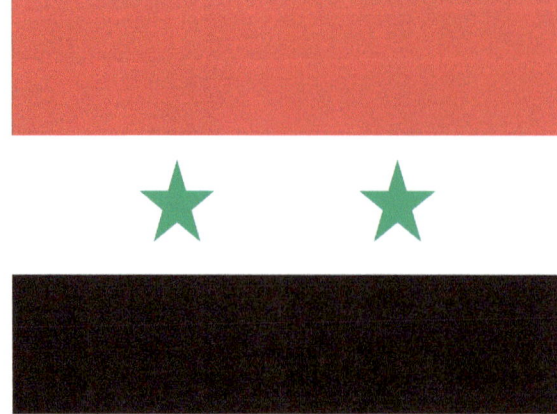

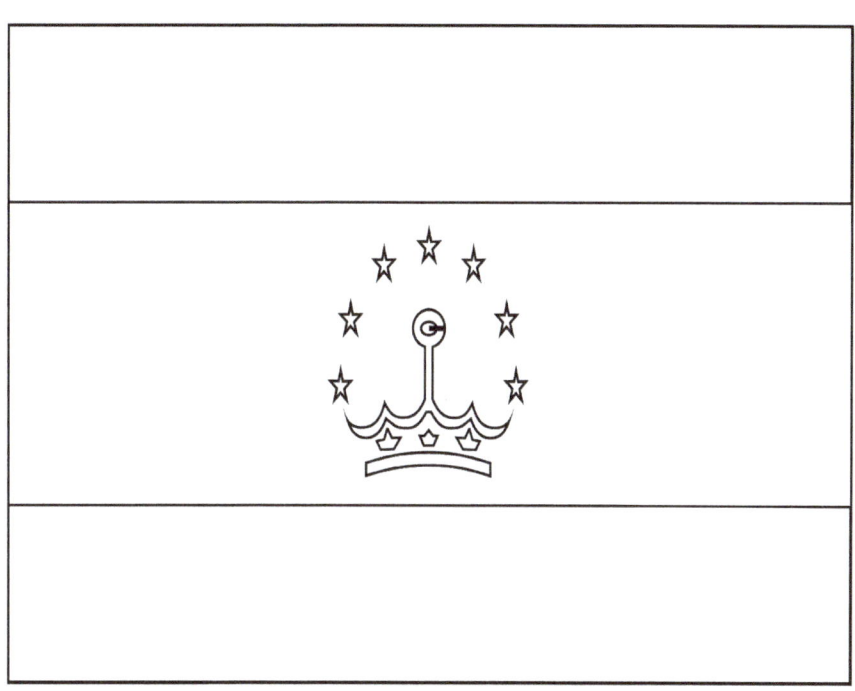

TAJIKISTAN

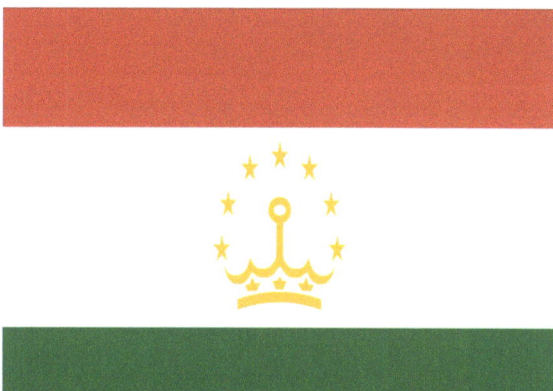

THAILAND

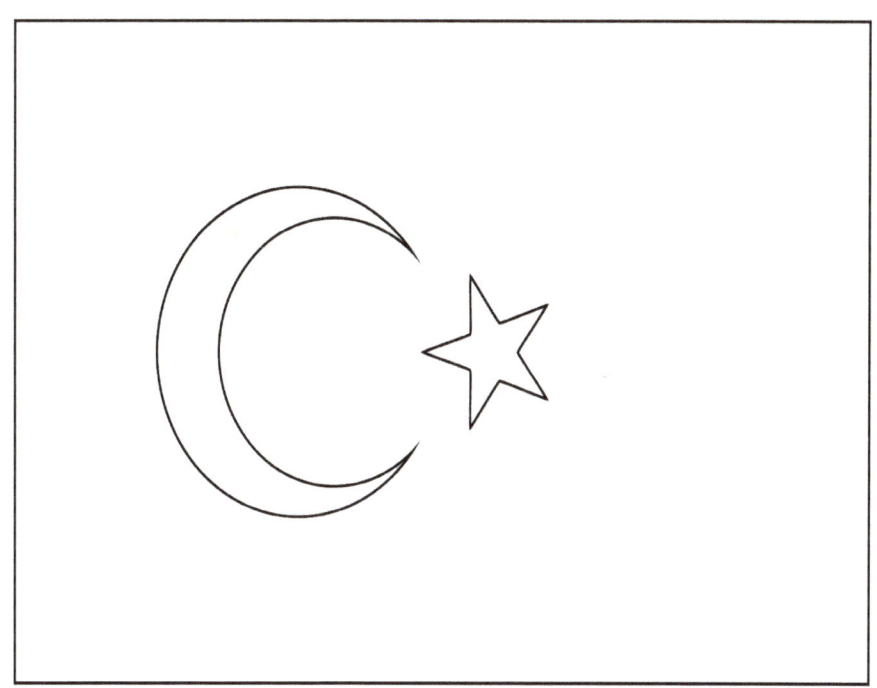

TURKEY

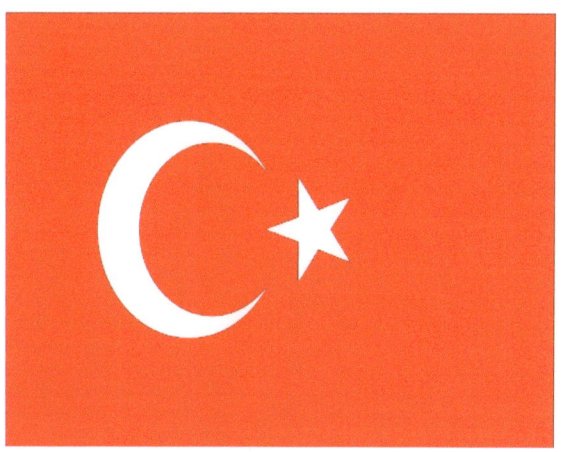

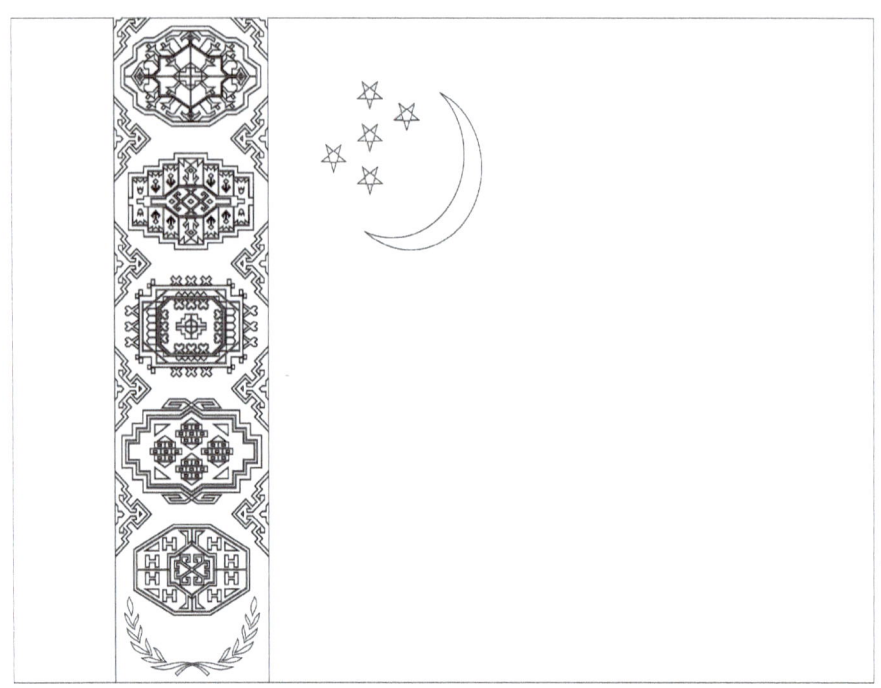

TURKMENISTAN

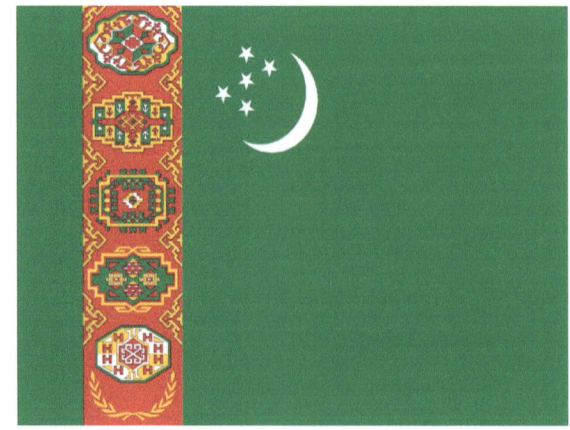

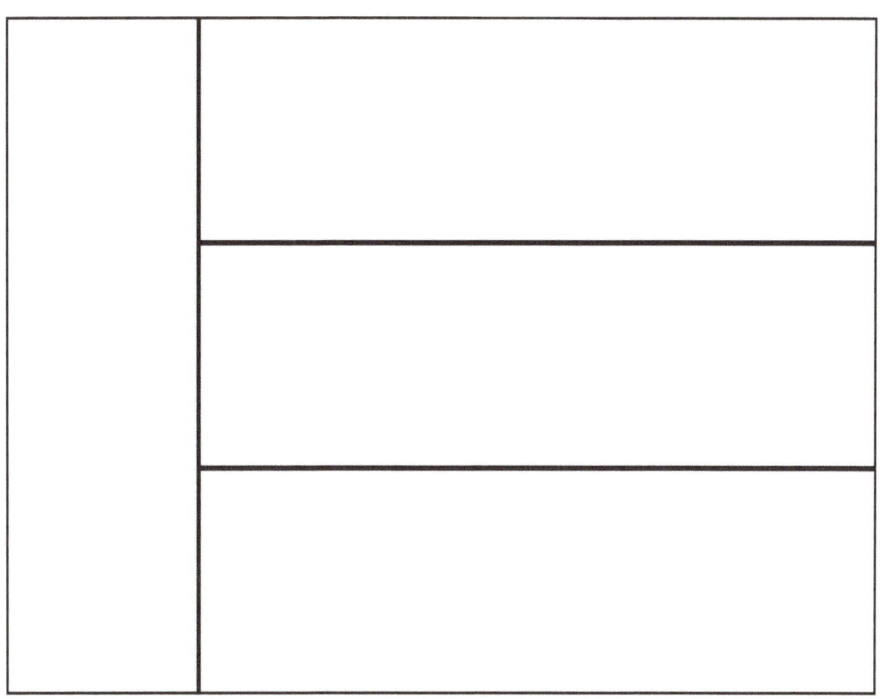

UNITED ARAB
EMIRATES

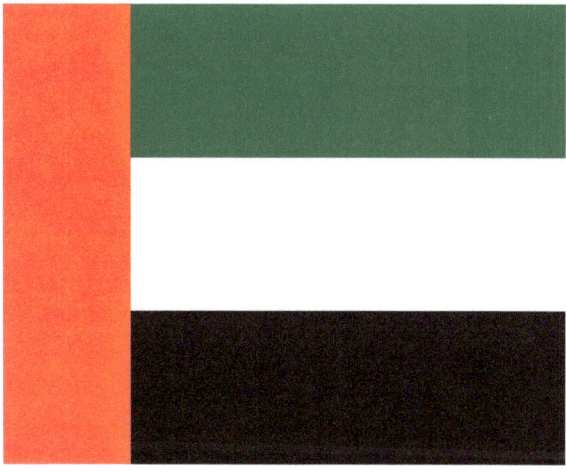

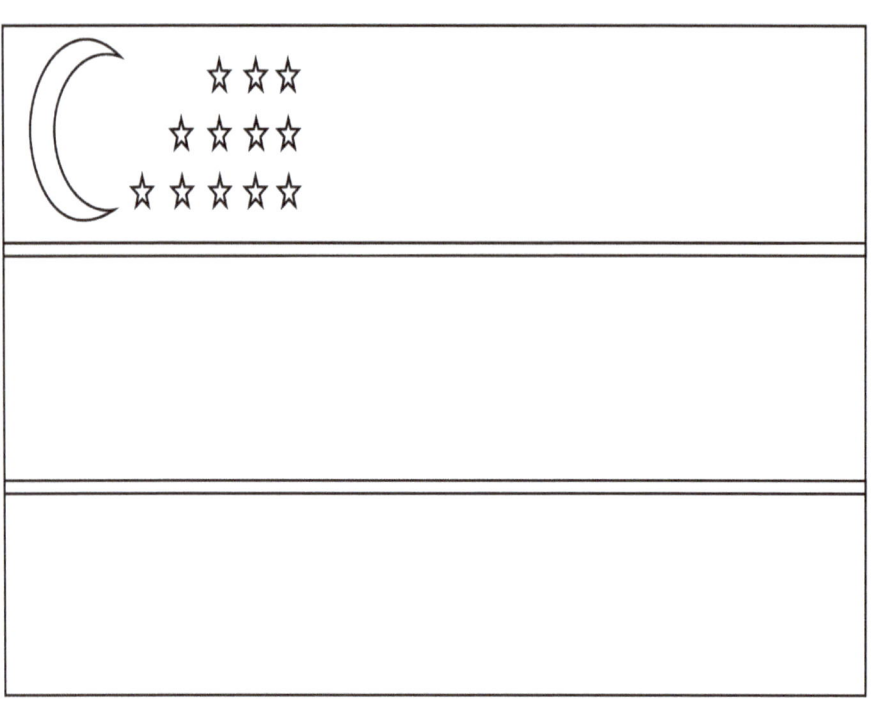

UZBEKISTAN

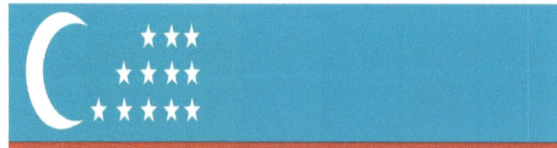

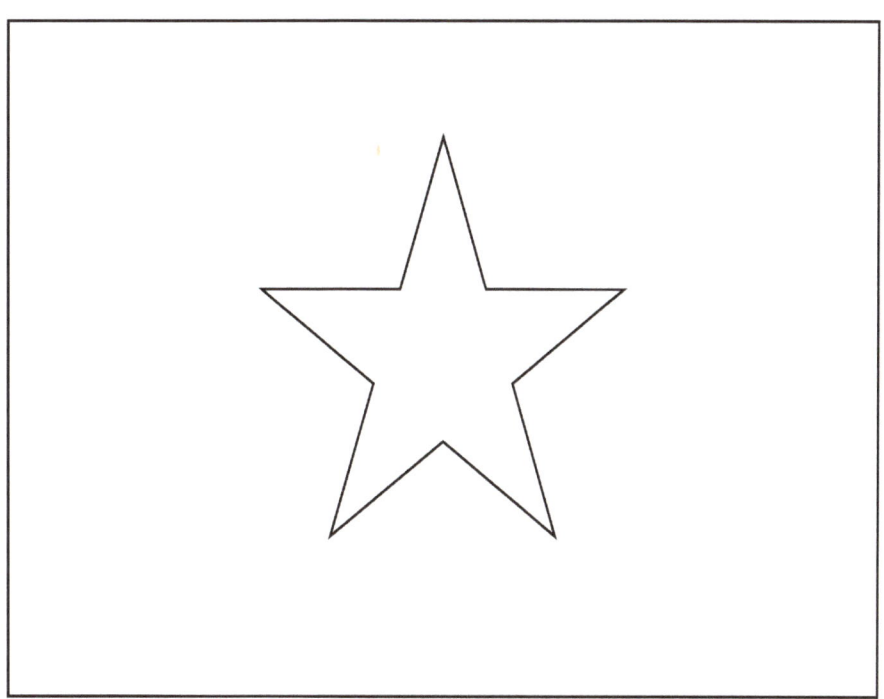

VITENAM

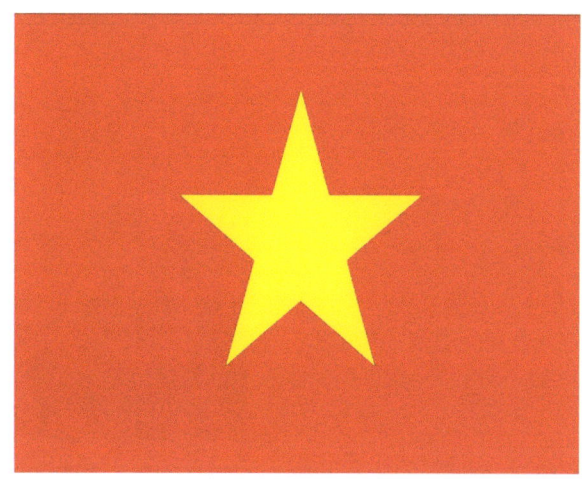

YEMEN

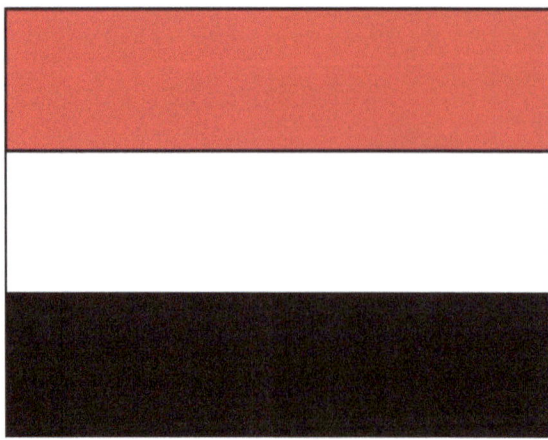